Democratic Oak Tree

Messages for My Party

JONATHAN BAYLISS

DRAWBRIDGE PRESS

2016

Published by Drawbridge Press
www.DrawbridgePress.com
PO Box 833
Gloucester MA 01931

ISBN 978-0-9831504-8-0 (paper)

Contents

Publisher's Note vii

◻ *1952* ◻   *1*
That Great & Fine Adlai Stevenson

◻ *1976* ◻   *3*
I Was Wrong!!

◻ *1980* ◻   *4*
Deserves Unstinting Credit
Guff without Reason or Mercy

◻ *1982* ◻   *5*
Republicans Remain So Far Ahead in the Senate

◻ *1984* ◻   *6*
Failed Another Test

◻ *1986* ◻   *6*
Much More Catholic Attitude toward Society
If the Republicans Keep Control of the Senate

◻ *1990* ◻   *10*
Interesting for Depressing Reasons

◻ *1991* ◻   *10*
Registered?

◻ *1992* ◻   *10*
How Important Discredit Really Is

◻ *1994* ◻   *10*
Tactful Allusions to Our Politics

□ *1997* □   *12*

Balanced Budget Amendment □ Covert Tax Motives

□ *1998* □   *15*

Definition of "Sexual Intercourse"

□ *1999* □   *16*

State of the Union □ Why Your Political Party Is Important □ Their Self-Righteousness □ Clinton Deserves Sympathy and Support □ Rousing Speech on "Single-Payer" Health Plans □ Clinton and Albright □ Gore Is Going to Surprise □ It's the Party That Makes the Difference

□ *2000* □   *21*

Remember What Happened to McGovern □ Clinton Remains the Benign Giant □ Republicans Trumpet Their Faith □ Helms □ As President You Have to Deal with Everything □ It's Parties That Get Things Done □ The Base of My Politics □ "A Necessary Evil" □ Step-By-Step Compromises □ Importance of Any Politician's Party Affiliation □ If Unions Are Prohibited □ Ingrained (Quasi-Legal) Corruption □ My Most Personally Beloved Politician □ Who Needs Political Parties? □ Nader May Make the Difference □ Psychological Insight on the Part of Voters □ Electoral Weight □ Election Will Make a Great Negative Difference □ The Folly of His Naderism

□ *2001* □   *41*

Loyalty to Clinton-Gore □ Ashcroft Is Worse □ Post-Bellum Sweet-Talk with Stiletto Up the Sleeve □ The South Is Rising in DC □ Larger Immoralities of Money and Power □ The Plutocratic Party □ Looking for New Democratic Hero □ Spiritual Selfishness □ New and Old Democrats □ Big Play for the Catholic Vote □ Gore Deserves Sympathy Instead of Scorn □ FDR and Clinton Always Understood

¤ *2002* ¤   *50*

Number One Political Task ¤ In Greater Political Danger ¤ Only Bulwark against Bush ¤ I Fear Trent Lott ¤ City Charter Commission ¤ Deceived by Hope ¤ Residual Prejudice against Women in Power ¤ The Big Lie ¤ Taking Advantage of Dixiecrat Emotions ¤ Al Gore Has Just Dropped Out of 2004 ¤ General Philosophy for the Common Good

¤ *2003* ¤   *61*

War Only If and When Necessary ¤ Emphasize Gore's Proven Reputation ¤ Pounding Away at Bush's Economic Folly and Injustice ¤ Wartime Macho-Sentimentality ¤ Degradation of the Democratic Dogma ¤ Why Sign Up as a Democrat? Thoughts for Recruiting ¤ Party That Has Obstructed Justice ¤ Some Abstract Thought ¤ Partisan Voting ¤ What If Maggie Were Still in Charge? ¤ Gore and Clark ¤ Mistaking Bush as an Honorable Gentleman ¤ As Unassailable as a Liberal Can Get ¤ Tax Cuts for Rich People Have a Dual Purpose ¤ Gore's Speech ¤ Gore and Clark ¤ 1000% Superior to George II's ¤ Tree-Root Politics ¤ A New American Patriotism ¤ Achievement in Diplomacy ¤ Losing Substantial Confidence in Blair ¤ Moral Courage as a Keenly Responsible Leader ¤ Coming Election Is Our One Hope ¤ A Few Pins and Stickers ¤ Debt and Deception ¤ Concern for the International Environment

¤ *2004* ¤   *87*

Clark's Strength as a Leader ¤ Toward True Philosophical Patriotism ¤ Our Only Hope ¤ A Candidate Who Can Win Over a Majority ¤ The Real Issue about the War ¤ It's the Salesman's Duplicity ¤ Would Make a World-Respected Team ¤ Must Keep Singing WKC's Praises ¤ If We Are to Save Civilization and Mother Earth ¤ Temperamentally a Meliorist ¤ Convention Served Its Purpose ¤

Practical Politics Is Party Politics ¤ Their Grand Plan for an "Ownership Society" ¤ Apotheosis of Selfishness ¤ Crocodile Tears about Integrity in Journalism ¤ Define the Common Good ¤ Kerry Has Guts ¤ Economic Social Justice ¤ Don't Blame Kerry

¤ *2005* ¤   *107*
Individual vs. Society ¤ Our Political Philosophy ¤ Bush Is Pure Salesman ¤ Kick from an Old Donkey ¤ Crucial Need for a Political Philosophy ¤ Second Kick from an Old Donkey ¤ A Political Philosophy That Will Win Elections ¤ The One Great Idea ¤ The Widening Economic Gap

¤ *2006* ¤   *123*

The Makings of a Political Philosophy ¤ Worried (for 2008) about McCain

¤ *2007* ¤   *125*
Centralized Voting

¤ *2008* ¤   *126*
We Have Hillary

Chronology   *127*

Index   *131*

*About
the Author*   *135*

Publisher's Note

This collection of letters, essays, newspaper pieces, and email messages – with opinions about more than a half century of American politics, Democratic vs. Republican values, Democratic candidates, Presidential elections, and advice to Democrats and voters – is offered in lieu of the book that Jonathan Bayliss (1926-2009), novelist and playwright, would have published if he hadn't run out of time. If he had lived another year or two, he would have written – as he had intended – a whole book about politics. He was determined to finish the final volume of his fiction tetralogy *Gloucesterman* first.

The meat of this little volume will be found in the more formal expositions of Bayliss's views in the following essays:

> Why Your Political Party Is Important (1999)
> Who Needs Political Parties (2000)
> New and Old Democrats (2001)
> Why Sign Up as a Democrat (2003)
> Tree-Root Politics (2003)
> Our Political Philosophy (2005)
> Kick From an Old Donkey (2005)
> Second Kick from an Old Donkey (2005)
> The One Great Idea (2005)
> The Makings of a Political Philosophy (2006)

The side offerings, taken from personal correspondence, include sometimes repetitive political commentary mixed in with intellectual subjects. The allusions to religion and popular culture may be distasteful or at least questionable to some readers but offer food for thought to others. In Bayliss's communications, Democrats are sometimes called Catholicrats ("Crats") and Republicans Protesticans ("Cans"). The confusing historical ties between politics and religion are a theme in Bayliss's novels as well.

Most of the messages are included in their entirety; they contain personal tidbits that may be pushed aside or perhaps relished.

A brief chronology is given at the back of this volume to refresh memories about elections from 1952 to 1998.

A steadfast Democrat, Bayliss was pleased to have lived, as he expressed it, between the bookends of FDR and Barack Obama.

Those who share hopes for a better society – who believe in providing for the "general Welfare" and working for the Common Good – may find some encouraging ideas in the pages that follow.

2016

October 11, 1952

To Richard Green

That Great & Fine Adlai Stevenson

I wish I could take more time to answer your long, kind letter. But I'd be using all my non-business energy (even if sometimes only in the form of nervous energy) for that great & fine Adlai Stevenson.

I hope I am not presumptuous in assuming that you are now a firmer Democrat than ever.

My delight & enthusiasm has its price in proportionate (and alternate) despair. One evening I go to bed early as an escape from the ugly depression of a futile day in the national campaign (– so it seems), or from too compelling an association with the all-powerful spirit of Republicanism; the next day I go to bed early because I'm too excited with history-conscious optimism to be able to read.

All life, except for the perfunctory hours at the office,* is suspended in this violently undulating fever. My mind is too little brave to be able to think – in my heart – of DEFEAT; the conception of it is appalling both from the positive result of it in the form of a Republican government and from the fear of wasting the *finest* (combining intention with ability) public servant of the century. Perhaps I go too far; nevertheless, I think, Wilson never had such access to success, and Roosevelt never had such an affinity for what is *absolutely* fine in the highest of cultural development. He'll be personally less successful than Roosevelt, I doubt not, but he'll leave an immediate political heritage that will preserve the New Deal objectives without destroying the aristocratic privilege of metaphysics. Stevenson's political philosophy is not a vulgar humanism that will exalt sociology and drive original sin underground.

I'm a fool to harangue *you*! I started out merely to send you the enclosed reprint. Please pass it on to a doubtful vote. New Jersey is just barely hopeful enough so that I know I'm not wasting it!

As for myself, I avail myself of all the little displays of publicity that are otherwise categorically distasteful – buttons, car stickers, etc. I am doing precinct work, making ingratiating phone calls & visits to registered Democrats. There's a democrat under every rock; our problem in Calif. is to expose them to the light – and many of them have been in obscurity thirsting for it. How surprised they are to find Alameda has a Stevenson club!

By a series of lucky chances I saw, heard, & *literally* brushed shoulders with Mr. S. at his last appearance in S.F. Wednesday we turn out for his next – at a big, old-fashioned rally at the Cow Palace.

All Berkeley – the part we have known as well as the part along San Pablo – shares my practical interest. Teaching Assistants are ringing doorbells; lecturers are soliciting money; professors (–this I know only by hearsay) have spontaneously raised a campaign fund.

I hope every University is the same way. The academic profession, adding all the bits, can indeed be formidable on behalf of the good as well as for the spiritually mediocre.

You must have the same feeling I have – that, for a few months at least, the political energy can comprehend within itself the symbols of the absolute dualism.** This "pragmatical pig of a world" is not too much with Stevenson; yet it is within his control. Under Stevenson the highly dogmatic Catholic and the wretched artist will be equal with the psychologist and the economist before a suprahumanistic law.

As usual I get carried away! Stevenson can't be *that* wonderful! There are certain vulgarities in *everyone*'s life. It's so rarely I can give complete allegiance that when I do so I have to yield on faith a thoroughgoing respect on every level. I like to think that I would respect the man as a philosopher & literary critic above all other philosophers & literary critics! But I don't go so far as to call him a hero! Still, my emotional absurdity carries me away from my private work long enough to help get him elected. On no other terms could

I throw to the winds three months of precious literature (incoming & outgoing).

What you say about contemporary literature's alternative "contentment" (about things known or not known as they are) strikes me as exactly just. I hope I'll never be drawn into that out of artistic superficiality. It is *not* superficial (philosophically, artistically speaking) only during such months as these – when there should be no questions, after all, of mankind's essential disturbances. Eisenhower's quasi-wickedness is no less close to truth, I suppose, than Truman's quasi-goodness. And Stevenson's Unitarian catholicism is probably no closer to the truth than William James and his brother. But it's hard for me now – what with a life of business, politics, and family – to keep sight of what my life and yours is really worth.

At my best – those rare times! – even the Catholics are to me relatively humanistic. Even Kierkegaard!

Please tell me, watchman, what of New Jersey?

* Two temporary exceptions: World Series; Cal's weekly football.

** In my sense. Perhaps not in yours. Even the Manichaeans are not absolutely absolute about it. (In one sense, I'm not too!)

November 3, 1976
To Victoria Bayliss Mattingly

I Was Wrong!!

It's your birthday and I write you with the same heavy heart about the world's future that I had the night before Stevenson was to be defeated by Eisenhower. It's your bad luck to be associated with political disaster – especially this year, which was the last chance for Americans to disprove the decline once and for all of history. But I'm glad we're away from television. We're as insulated as we can be from the immediacy of truth.

[postmarked Southampton, England, November 8, with note on back of envelope:] I WAS WRONG!!

February 8, 1980

Letter to editor, *Gloucester Daily Times*

Deserves Unstinting Credit

Since I have been mentioned as a dissenter, I'd like to explain my lone vote against the pre-primary endorsement of Senator Kennedy for president by the Gloucester Democratic City Committee.

I am not against Kennedy. I consider him one of the great senators of the twentieth century. He has eloquently and consistently and vigorously advocated policies and programs I support. I hope he will become Jimmy Carter's successor in 1984.

Meanwhile I vote for Carter positively. He deserves unstinting credit for making the moral imperative of human rights an essential element of American foreign policy; for his vital part in establishing true peace between Israel and Egypt, one of the most skillful such achievements in the history of international relations; and in general for demonstrating to the world that American values are more than merely "pragmatic."

I admire President Carter's exceptional ability to grasp extremely complex problems, and especially his willingness to attack the underlying managerial problems of government that other presidents rarely even attempt to understand, difficulties that are largely unreported or unrecognized by the press upon which the public depends for its appreciation of the presidency. In the long run it's management that makes or breaks any program, any policy. But it takes more than four years to reform the vast federal apparatus of bureaucracy and legislation.

Perhaps for liberals the president's proposals are not ideal. But they are progressive – and progressive at a time when conflicting forces seem to paralyze a weakened Congress more conservative than he is. No human being, no hero, can look good as chief executive while his nation is undergoing an historically inevitable experience of sudden limitations. It is much easier to whip a country into dramatic action than it is to foster a new kind of patriotism. The very fact that Jimmy Carter is being blamed for all the ills of the world by both liberals and conservatives at least suggests that we should try to appreciate this new kind of leader.

August 31, 1980

To Victoria Bayliss Mattingly

Guff without Reason or Mercy

... But I can't seem to worry about personal matters. It's the world and the American electorate that I get depressed about: especially the stupidity of experts and academic historians who can't see history in front of their faces (re: Pres. Carter). If Carter wins it will be in spite of his abilities – not because of them. He might as well run on an anti-Reagan basis, since he's getting all the anti-Carter guff without reason or mercy. It's the "Intellectuals" of this country that enrage me most. We and Israel, both, are just reliving the moral disasters of the Old Testament.

November 3, 1982

To Victoria Bayliss Mattingly

Republicans Remain So Far Ahead in the Senate

I remember the political consequence (post hoc non propter hoc) of your original birthday: Adlai Stevenson lost the election in which we hoped against hope for victory. Now today his son has lost (apparently). So it's a good year again – it must be, somehow, even though we've just lost almost every one of the close elections from Rhode Island to California and the Republicans remain so far ahead in the Senate that 1984 will be extremely difficult for a Democratic President, if we get one. But many things come out well, so I shouldn't complain about the consequence of your 30th. (In fact, I should have written this on time, beforehand, before there were any results.) ...

November 26, 1984

To Victoria Bayliss Mattingly

Failed Another Test

... The American people have failed another test. I hope it won't be their last one. But I get the feeling that the country feels a little ashamed of what it's done. The day after the election the Deficit projection went up again. But if they didn't learn about Republicans from Nixon, I'm afraid they won't from Reagan either. They are as foolish as the Bander-Log being swallowed by Kaa. ... I thought of you on your birthday, my dear child of '52 (the year of my greatest *political* disappointment), and I hope it isn't too late to say that I love you.

January 23, 1986

To Peter DuBrul

Much More Catholic Attitude toward Society

I'm still experimenting with my "word processor". Please make allowances.

It's been almost four years since I spoke of *Clarel* (which I was just starting) and you gave me *The Great Code.* Much has intervened – Geoffrey's accident, two years+ in City Hall, etc., and a lot of other books that were in my way – but I was working at them all along, in parallel, intermittently, and I've just finished them both. It's an inefficient way to read, especially when one's memory is as bad as mine, but it's the most useful way for me. And *The Great Code* is a very very useful book for my continuing education, alongside *Clarel* in particular, as I work on my second unpublishable novel.

I know that I've already beset you with a screed about *Clarel*, but let me just emphasize that only a man of leisure with a monstrous appetite could get through it without Bezanson's copiously annotated edition. With proper preparation and assistance, and tolerance for technical imperfections in an outmoded convention of verse, it's extremely rewarding for anyone interested in Melville and/or American literature and/or Israel and/or Christianity. I'd like to send you a copy, if you'll give me an address I can count on for parcel post, unless you already have it or are at present too much on the wing.

HM was half secretly attracted to the RC Church at a time when it was unthinkable to the society he lived in. (I recently read that A N Whitehead also was, at Cambridge, and actually went to visit Cardinal Newman when Newman was very old; but with Whitehead it was apparently either/or, and he finally decided he was an agnostic instead: he simply couldn't stay where he'd been brought up, devotedly, with the Anglicans.) He was also anomalously sympathetic to the Jews, or at least to the Zionists. The whole poem seems to me a summation of all HM's works in which he directly faces the Catholic/Protestant conflict which lies undetected under all our politics and culture. (I speak under the persuasion of Tawney's *Religion and the Rise of Capitalism,* in terms of social morality.) In HM's time there was little contest, the country being almost officially Protestant, but since FDR (at least until the Republicans gained back some of their ground) we've lived with a much more Catholic attitude toward society, as something of value for its own sake, notwithstanding the intellectual confusion that keeps many Democrats Protestant and makes many Catholics Republican – a philosophical confusion hardly confined to America or American literature. I read many other writers (Yeats, for instance) as agonists in this unwitting cultural conflict.

Frye too! His book is the best I've ever read about the Bible, and it makes me appreciate a lot of things for the first time (like the Book of Job). It's a wonderful integration of literature and religion, and of both with the true advances of 20C cultural anthropology, archaeology, et al. It's as if he's grasped the *true* mythology.

But it's another near miss – a miss as good as a mile – because it almost totally ignores the ritual that underlies the myth, the liturgy that underlies even the Gospel. At bottom, he's too literary – a man of the word more than a man of the *action* – to escape the Protestant bias. I'd like to see someone take us through the Bible as a history of the groping and finally triumphant discovery (through Christ's demonstration) of *successful* sacrifice.

One of the saddest facts in the world today, to me, is that even the churchmen of Liberation Theology (as far as I've read about it) don't make the logical connection that humanity is unconsciously athirst for: between liturgy and the *quality of society* (whether it's capitalist or socialist being a subsidiary matter of instrumental argument) – the optimum survival of the species. This sacramental technology of the liturgy (as distinguished from its necessary but insufficient symbolism, which by itself is not essentially distinguishable from that of other mythologies) seems to be an embarrassment even to the Conference of Bishops. It's as if the liturgy, rather than being central to Christianity, were some more or less arbitrary personal and private discipline of the Church's that the rest of the world should indulge, equivalent to the ceremonial customs that comfort people emotionally all the world over: but pay no attention to it – it doesn't stand in the way of our political perception and goodwill! The argument for peace and reform and justice is based only on the purely moral exhortations common to all people of goodwill trying to live up to the Gospel without using the sine qua of practical grace that Jesus went to great pains to provide us – or else simply upon obedience to God's general commandments, just to please God. Then why bother with the Church?

I realize that my attitude must seem grossly physical, technological, anti-pietistic, non-"spiritual": but I think of it as reducing the mystery to its irreducible sacrament, which provides everyone who is pious and spiritual with the rational nexus to their instinctive or charitable social yearnings. I don't think the species can be reformed or even saved from self-destruction without the divine help that we can get collectively only by one particularly ordained method, which should be explained to the world, as the Bible is now explained by people like Frye.

Anyway, I'm very grateful for the book, and I wanted to explain why I didn't read it immediately as I promised. I had a lot of collateral reading to do to do it justice, including some of the Bible itself, which I'd read through without much comprehension and otherwise knew only from readings in church (which are of course out of direct context) and from the few books of it that I've searched out from time to time in connection with particular interests. But it's one of the parallel tracks I try not to stand still on. My next related project will be the *Gnostic Gospels,* which I expect to find will reinforce my anti-gnosticism. Have you read it yet?

By the way, I think the Tawney book serves as the exact touchstone for interpreting our present political situation. Do you admire it as much as I do?

Please excuse my over-reaction. It shows how isolated I feel in seeing the barn door that's transparent to everyone else! I hope this finds you with enough leisure to peruse this floundering stab at trying to articulate what I mean.

Yours incoherently, with the hope that your work prospers in that unique place. *Clarel* has made me wish to see and touch the stones you live among.

September 15, 1986
To Joseph Mattingly

If the Republicans Keep Control of the Senate

... The reactionary momentum will gather exponentially in the next two years if the Republicans keep control of the Senate, and Iowa is one of the key states. It's painful to witness the indifference of any American to party politics (the only kind that's effective). ...

November 3, 1990
To Victoria Bayliss Mattingly
Interesting for Depressing Reasons

... Otherwise there's nothing going on here except politics, which has become very interesting for depressing reasons ...

November 3, 1991
To Victoria Bayliss Mattingly
Registered?

... Have you registered to vote? Can you run for office? ...

April 15, 1992
To Victoria Bayliss Mattingly
How Important Discredit Really Is

... The political picture, after some hope, is discouraging. I'm afraid Bush is going to pull off the same intempestive trick that John Major did, just because the Dems. aren't going to nominate Cuomo. The "conservatives" are all discredited, but the cultural lag due to journalism prevents the public from seeing how important discredit really is ...

February 10, 1994
To the Rev Philip J Lee (author of *Against the Protestant Gnostics*)
Tactful Allusions to Our Politics

I came across your book in a casual perusal of an Oxford catalog and ordered it for the title alone, which seemed to promise food in the wilderness! And it did: manna. Perhaps by now my kind of response to it is too familiar to you – after five or more years – to be interesting, but the book is so stimulating that I can't refrain from this fan letter.

I hope your book stays in print forever. Have you a subsequent book, or any other published writings on American culture or historical religion? Your tactful allusions to our politics should be amplified and brought up to date! Our new President I would call a Protestant Antignostic. At this moment he's fighting all the gnostics at once, without as much help as he should have from socially misguided Catholics – whose own insidious gnosticism you even more tactfully avoid.

I especially appreciate your symmetrical treatment of rightwing and leftwing (syncretic) heresies. The religious-political correspondence is totally ignored in our journalism, as if historical ideology had no bearing on current events, either here, in Britain, or in Bosnia. I read somewhere that Maggie Thatcher said: "There's no such thing as society: there's only the individual and the family." The truth is that most Americans also don't believe in society. Certainly Reagan and Bush didn't. In this country the only institution (if it can barely be called such) that opposes gnostic individualism in political economy is the Democratic Party, though it does so partially, inconsistently, and for the most part unconsciously. I often think that we have the most naive electorate in the democratic world. Our people believe in Disney imagery, and in the magic of computers (while ignorant and indifferent to knowledge of real science and technology), as perfectly continuous extensions of the gnosticism-vs-sacramentalism you discuss.

Yet you have overcome my Anglo-catholic prejudice against *orthodox* Protestantism, which I had been inclined to think was *all* gnostic! I was amazed at how catholic your position is. The "accomplishment" of the liturgy seems to be the only real issue, not the importance of it. I would love to read your historical critique of the Catholic side.

Which brings me to the other reason I'm writing. Your basic social-sacramental argument might very well have been made in large part by my old friend Father Elmer Smith, lately of the C of E parish in Prince William, N B. As I understand it, he led a Diocese of Fredericton 1972 revision of the liturgy as a Trial Eucharistic Rite, which I think you would find congenial. (He was a member of the tiny, now defunct, Episcopalian Society of the Catholic Commonwealth.) I've been hoping that you knew him, or still know him if he's still alive.

Anyway, if I get a chance to travel up that way this year I'd like very much to call on you. In any case you have my gratitude, and I'm doing my best to promulgate your book among my friends, almost all of whom are seduced by some form of gnosticism, of which the worst is Jungian. Have you had much encouragement from outfits like the Harvard Divinity School?

January 24, 1997

To Anthony Lewis, *New York Times*

Balanced Budget Amendment

I was very glad to see your column today. Most journalists don't seem to read the text, or to appreciate its significance.

This is one objective that the Republicans have been doggedly consistent about, all through these last four years, because the root of it is their inveterate resistance to taxation. At one point less than a year ago Gingrich even admitted that balancing the budget immediately wasn't all-important. They object to debt and deficit mainly because it threatens the tax bills of themselves and their principal constituents. Even more covertly than overtly they have been whipping up specious sentiment for this amendment because of the paragraphs that follow the first one.

I haven't been able to find the present text of the Senate proposal but it may still include a provision that is even more pernicious than the one you mention – namely, the one restricting increases of revenue. An earlier version in the House required a 60% vote to raise taxes – but only a majority would remain necessary to lower them!

This is their dearest wish. All they'd have to do is get control for two years in order to reduce taxes. Then later, even in a minority of 40% (which they'll probably always have), they would be able to block progressive taxation until there's a national emergency.

I believe that a later version corrected this original asymmetry but I have been unable to find the full text of the version that will be voted on this year. I hope you will write again on this subject, which is the most important constitutional issue of our time – especially because it would sweep through the state legislatures on sheer sentimental grounds.

What I find disheartening about all the other pundits is their omission of motivational analysis – as if the two parties were two football teams playing for the same goals – with the same set of values. They talk about ad hoc "policies" and "programs" without trying to understand what motivates the individuals who promote them. (Item, the conservationists vs the environmental free-wheelers – as if there were no psychological difference between altruism and self-aggrandizement.)

Of course the core Republicans exploit other motives, and get many of their votes for coadjutant reasons; but since long before FDR called them "economic royalists" the GOP has been consciously and subconsciously based on tax resistance. They regard this constitutional amendment proposal as the chance of a lifetime.

I realize that there are plenty of other serious difficulties with their proposal (including sheer impracticability), which at last are beginning to be debated in public. But Republicans have more votes this time. I hope you'll continue to weigh in, and, if you see fit, discuss the Trojan Horse of taxation. (Section 4?)

At least please urge your colleagues to publicize the full text of the proposed balanced budget amendment.

January 29, 1997

To *Boston Globe* Editorial Page

Covert Tax Motives

I was very glad to see your column in today's *Globe*. I hope you will write more on this pernicious proposal.

It's a Trojan horse full of separable problems.

So far almost all the public debate has been concentrated on the first section of the resolution in Congress. But I'd like to call your special attention to Section 2, which concerns the all-important issue of taxes. Nothing is as important to Republicans as their covert tax-motives.

Sen Gramm's version calls for a 60+% vote to raise taxes. Note that it would still take only a majority vote to lower taxes. Let us assume that the Republicans will always have at least 40% of Congress. When they are in power, as they are now, they can lower taxes. But then when in the minority later they could block any increase in taxes. (This would be comparable to having a permanent majority on the Supreme Court!)

Here's one of the ironies: If a House version of this Section passes which requires only the usual majority to raise taxes, the entire BBA could backfire on the Republicans, because in a serious recession, with public opinion demanding more, not less, government spending, Congress would be forced to raise taxes – especially on the rich – which is the very last thing in the world the Republicans want!

I wish the *Globe* would print the various texts. (It is not very good on simple facts. I had to buy the World Almanac even to find the complete membership of the new Senate.)

The best thing, of course, is to defeat the whole BBA. But the next best thing would be to defeat the Three Fifths requirement in Section 2 (and in Section 6 on raising the debt).

I earnestly request that you call public attention to this and other neglected clauses of the BBA. Judging by Clinton's remarks yesterday

I'm not sure even he is paying enough attention to Section 2 – but that may be a matter of political prudence, since the very word TAXES can scare people at every level. But how can Joe Kennedy and Meehan support such a regressive meddling with the Constitution?

Have they thought it through?

We need you more than ever. "Conservatism" is all the rage. No one any longer dreams of calling the Republicans "economic royalists".

December 22, 1998

To David Kendall, Esq. (Counsel, White House)

Definition of "Sexual Intercourse"

This is to suggest a line of inquiry in defense of the President insofar as it may concern the charge of "lying under oath" about sexual matters.

I believe that you can get expert testimony from academic anthropologists about the definition of "sexual intercourse" corroborating Mr Clinton's interpretation of the questions directed to him. It appears that in the study of native life in American Samoa, for example, Margaret Mead and other social scientists defined sexual relations in similarly narrow terms.

And of course there have been millions of erotically experienced college students in previous generations (both male and female demi-vierges) who regarded themselves as fortunately or unfortunately innocent of sexual intercourse on the basis of just such "technicalities".

In any event, I think the President is well advised not to admit perjury in this regard, unless some agreement is reached that will protect him from further prosecution.

January 28, 1999
To Richard Altobelli

State of the Union

Reducing the debt saves interest costs, doesn't it? For that alone I'd be for it. But mainly because it puts the gov't in a better position to borrow when times are bad or in emergency. I don't believe in the optimistic fiscal projections anyway. For the sake of social justice and world peace and Mother Earth we should salt away all we can while the going's good!

January 31, 1999

Why Your Political Party Is Important

Maggie Thatcher says, "There's no such thing as society – only the individual and the family." Republicans agree. That usually means your own family and families like your own. You are kind to your own kind. You hardly consider the millions who have no families at all. Rugged individualism can be self-righteous, even spiritually and morally selfish. One of the chaplains at the 1996 Republican convention said "God wants us to be rich!"

In contrast, Democrats believe in society – the commonwealth, the common good of the nation and the world – as well as in the individual. There is more to true patriotism than glory and super-power.

But why is it important to join any Party?

The party represents a set of values. You may not agree with your party on a particular issue or policy, but you know the party's *general motive.* There is a solidarity of intention about economic and environmental problems, human rights, racial and gender equality – most of the aspects of planetary, social, and individual justice. You may not have time to join even one of the special causes you approve of; no one can be involved in them all. Many citizens are unable to attend political meetings. But by supporting the party with your name (and voting in all elections) you exert an influence far greater than that of an "independent". You can affect almost ALL the public issues you are interested in.

Above all, by helping to choose and elect a state or federal representative you gain the constitutional advantage of a full-time professional who serves most of your special interests in much greater depth and detail than you can possibly know as a private citizen. You have the leverage of being reinforced by all the others who vote for your candidate.

By joining a party you greatly multiply whatever contribution you make in money as well as votes. And you find yourself among friends.

February 6, 1999
To Gene Bailey

Their Self-Righteousness

Thanks for the covers.

As soon as Hamilton is ready to say, can you give me the case-weights and some sort of volume measurement (cu ft per thousand or per case) so that I can plan for storage?

...

The House Managers wouldn't let their own body see or hear before railroading the impeachment; then before the Senate they clamor for full public exposure. Their self-righteousness, I hope, will seem ludicrous to voters in 2000, and thereafter unto the third and fourth generation!

May 10, 1999

To Gene Bailey

Clinton Deserves Sympathy and Support

Thanks for the tip. It would eliminate the billing problem. We'll check on it later. The trouble is that we want to distribute to the trade, Amazon's virtual competitors. Catherine's going to work on the whole thing in a couple of weeks. Meanwhile the world of lead-balloon blockbusting will have to cool its heels.

I can hardly bear to listen to the news. Clinton deserves sympathy and support, not highminded criticism. I earnestly recommend Victor Klemperer's "I Will Bear Witness" (a diary which deserves the fame of Pepys or Ann Frank) for a day-by-day parallel of highminded appeasement in Hitler's day. Clinton has 19 legislatures to deal with, not just English and French suppliants and a minority in Congress. It is truly agonizing to argue with a sincere pacifist – more so than with insincere Republican militaristic isolationists (when there is no oil at stake).

May 18, 1999

To Gene Bailey

Rousing Speech on "Single-payer" Health Plans

When I returned from a 3-day weekend I found a lovely illustrated note from Lydia. She will obviously be a talented lady in the Bailey lineage.

Thanks also for the Beam clipping you had sent. Apparently a lot of people read Beam who are glad to read ABOUT me. It's like the dog who talks: everyone is so delighted when he speaks at all that they don't notice what he says.

Richard is asking about shipping cartons. I've been searching my email files but I can't find the message you sent me that identified the one you used. Wasn't it from Staples? Can you remember the catalog number? (I tried especially to preserve that message but I must have misplaced it with evil keystrokes. I'm sorry to bother you again about it.)

Gov Dean of Vt. gave a rousing speech on "single-payer" health plans at the State Convention. I was surprised at his political passion. (He's a doctor.) I was also very pleased with the warm ovation Dukakis got just as an introducer for someone else. Finneran got a few boos.

July 7, 1999
Letter to editor, *The New Yorker*

Clinton and Albright

At last a commentator who can see the woods, not just the trees! While others see only the little bad things, Mr Hertzberg sees the big good thing! He has the vision of a future historian.

Clinton and Albright, with consummate skill, without dominating Europe, have led it (as well as us) into a moral action that promises to relieve us of sole imperial responsibility in the future.

The President's private foibles have blinded almost all journalists to his stature as a great statesman.

September 6, 1999
To Gene Bailey

Gore Is Going to Surprise

The only trouble is that I don't think it's been any better at all since Tina left. Maybe it's too early to tell?

I think Al Gore is going to surprise a lot of people in the long grind. He seems solid. Sooner or later people may appreciate his experience and humor.

October 18, 1999

Letter to editor, *Boston Globe*

It's the Party That Makes the Difference

Eric Goldscheider is exactly right in believing the world's future environment to be the ultimately important issue in politics. I agree that Gore, the candidate who most cares about "green" policies, should make it ONE of his major themes.

But Mr Goldscheider damages his own cause by ignoring the overall spectrums of position that distinguish the two viable parties. The complaints that Democrats and Republicans are much alike arise from the necessities of compromise in final legislative voting, not from similarity of values or initial positions.

Like the disgracefully dangerous Republican vote on the Test Ban Treaty, the Republican attitude toward environmental treaties and controls reflects the metaphysics of American "conservatism".

The two parties should be judged by their executive orders, administrative appointments, and votes in Congress, not by their "moderate" speeches as candidates. Republicans, as a minority of the public, usually disguise their semi-conscious philosophy in order to win elections, but in office they almost consistently support their party when it comes down to questions of the common good. That's what makes parties effective, for better or for worse.

So also do Democrats support each other, as they too should. Therefore, if you want to protect the environment, vote for almost any Democrat. It's the Party that makes the difference in the real world. They aren't just two football teams playing in the same league by the same rules.

Don't blame Clinton and Gore for failing to overcome the Republican Congress, which was elected by voters who don't appreciate the importance of political parties. Two parties are exactly the right number to distinguish basic values as simply as possible. Single-minded hopefulness makes for lost causes.

January 8, 2000

To Manfred Hegemann

Remember What Happened to McGovern

Well, you sound cheerful enough. So far we've had no winter. As long as it keeps getting lighter I won't care what's coming.

Living in beautiful isolation you had more to worry about at the turn of the millennium. Did you see the international celebrations on TV? Most impressive. For the first time in history the world seemed momentarily unified. What other holiday has ever been so universal?

I highly recommend the castration. Dogs aren't as macho as you are (in their minds). I've presided over it several times. But don't wait: the younger the better. After a few weeks everyone will be more happy and relaxed.

Cathy and I would like to take Clio up to see you all sometime soon. But Clio has just developed an internal left-hind-leg injury that we must wait to heal, so that she can tussle with Harto without further injury.

She has fantastic strength and energy, though small for the breed. Her relations with me remain at the Dr Jekle–Mr Hyde level of bipolar disorder (ie, dependent upon circumstances), but I think they are imperceptibly ameliorating. She behaves very well on travels, especially with Cathy present.

... I have just stumbled upon Thos Mann's story "A Man and his Dog". It's beautiful! Such leisurely writing would never be permitted in the USA. The humor is deliciously unsentimental. (But I'm only half through it so far.) It's very perceptive about dogs yet not overly realistic as a work of art.

You or Brigitte have probably long since known it.

... You may find PROLOGOS easier than the other books because you can pick and choose what may interest you. (Read the fourth paragraph on the back cover.) It's a goldmine and/or coppermine and/or coalmine and/or slag heap, but you have to do a lot of panning or digging for the glorious fun of finding the wealth you weren't looking for. But I say again, you are not EXPECTED to read any of the assignments.

You will get an honorary A just for allowing the books self space.

.... Little by little (illusory or not) Haiti, Yugoslavia, and Ireland seem to be quieting down, relieving me of moral pressure to worry actively about Clinton's worries about foreign affairs. So also with Israel, which interests me mainly as the prehistoric link between Sumer and Greece, the reason I'd like to get a three-day look at its topography and architecture on my trip to Rhodes, Munich, and elsewhere late next summer.

It looks as if the Feers are going to be away from home when I get to Switzerland. That's a disappointment, but my schedule is fixed for two weeks in Rhodes the first half of August. Still, it's possible they'll have a change of plans. [By the way, please explain his familiar name Beat(?). Is it pronounced Bay-at? What's its derivation? He seems to have several first names.]

Toward the end of August there's a conference of the Society for the History of Technology in Munich, where I expect to meet a friend who'll drive me to Linz where he lives and teaches.

Do you and Brigitte have any travel plans? If Harto has been neutered we could probably take care of him here while you're away. Clio would LOVE it!

If it's still convenient for you, what do you think of our trip up to visit (assuming that Clio recovers use of her fourth foot)?

She could use the influence of a noble Companion Dog!

... Forbes is an unbelievable dinosaur. His solution of the "health care problem" is to let EVERYONE buy whatever coverage they want. The trouble is that he makes Bush seem human. The latter strikes me as much like Dan Quayle. McCain means well, but he's fundamentally the product of military-Republican-Protestant one-side-of-the-equation indoctrination.

He's not broadly enough educated to see the antitheses in his "conservatism".

I like Bradley for what he wants (and his wife is a scholar of German literature), but I don't think there's any possibility of getting it the way he proposes. Gore has been battered into wisdom by the ugly reality of Americans' political stupidity. Remember what happened to McGovern.

In practical politics (including Christian public morality) Clinton remains the giant of our times. I hope he finds a future PUBLIC service career (and not in Hollywood).

So you have some of my usual offhand opinions!

Please offer Brigitte my encouragement to bear up under your tyranny.

January 8, 2000
To Gene Bailey

Clinton Remains the Benign Giant

What a wonderful millennium present!

I've already read Bradamante a few of those sophisticated bedtime poems. She purrs to hear them. They really are highly educated works of art. So good that I can imagine even the models for them that I haven't known before! What a nice way it would be to teach literature by means of sympathetic parodies – and at the same time pay homage to the cat-gods.

I am very grateful for your thoughtful generosity.

... What a dinosaur Steve Forbes is! So narrowly stupid about social reality. The trouble is that he makes the vacuous Bush seem harmless. ... Much as I like what Bradley wants, I don't think there's any possibility of getting it the way he proposes. Gore has been battered into a sense of political realism. I remembered how excited I was about McGovern. A Republican got elected.

Private behavior aside, I think Clinton remains the benign giant of our times. I hope his public service will somehow continue. I'm afraid his wife's will be at least temporarily scotched.

Please convey my warmest wishes for the next thousand years to good Shirley. Meanwhile, keep me posted on YOUR socio-political insights. I always find them "supportive"!

January 17, 2000

To Manfred Hegemann

Republicans Trumpet Their Faith

... Clinton has been doing a lot of important environmental things lately, but they get only the back pages – while Republicans trumpet their faith in personal salvation! I hope we can agree on the Demo nominee, but if not, we're not divided on objectives. (The journalists neglect objectives, they are so mesmerized by "policy" and "leadership" and "gay rights" and "gaffs", etc. As if Republicans were just an opposing team in the same league, playing for the same goals as Democrats.)

Would Brigitte and/or you vote for Hillary if you were still in NY? Did you see the remarkable TV on Eleanor Roosevelt?

January 24, 2000

To Gene Bailey

Helms

I happened to see Holbrooke testifying before Helms and Biden after the UN meeting. Holbrooke is very impressive. He and Albright invited him to the UN just to get the argument out in the open. Given the rules of the Senate, semi-conversion of Helms (or at least taming) is the only hope. By giving him a chance to spout off face-to-face to the whole UN they publically recognized his ego but also let him bear the burden of the organizational (managerial) criticism of the UN, some of which seems valid. That's a possible way of diverting a little of Helms' animus from the most important policy issues, especially to the extent of loosening our purse strings. (Don't forget that Biden, apparently, agrees with Helms about the dues adjustments, which seem to me reasonable, as long as we pay up the arrears. Some other nations also agree that 25% is too much because many new members have joined since that figure was set many years ago.)

I too hate dealing with the devil, but it seems to me better than stalemate, as long as there's a quid pro quo that moves in the right general direction. Otherwise we have to wait to get control of the Senate, which is said to be very unlikely this year.

PS: Is it any more disgusting than having to deal with Arafat or IRA or Ian Paisley or, for that matter, the Chinese or even (sometimes) the French?

If I hadn't happened to turn on C-Span at that moment I would have agreed with you 100%. And after all I did not see or read Helms's UN speech.

Am I getting too soft in my old age?

January 27, 2000
To Gene Bailey

As President You Have to Deal with Everything

I agree with all points below. I don't especially like the British psycho-violent detective stuff. Most of it makes no sense at all when you come to the end of the day. I never took up Fawlty Towers because I thought it was the department store nonsense, but next time around I will. (We get three PBS stations.) To me Ballykissangel is totally enthralling and I don't mind repetitions of it!

Can you imagine that, as President, Bradley would solve the Irak problem by TALKING the Arabs out of their oil production limits! It sounds like a Republican debating triumph. As a Senator you can pick and choose what to take an interest in; as President you have to deal with EVERYTHING in the world! You'd never hear Clinton or Gore give an answer like that. Even Bush Senior isn't that simple-minded.

And of course Bradley, with more experience as an executive, would never over-simplify, because he has the education and intelligence to make the most of experience. These "debate" questions are nothing but gauntlets that do little to test operational ability. I think that's one reason that party politics is so important: you know pretty well the intellectual company they'll keep if they get elected.

Anyway, thanks to Clinton, Gore has been in the thick of complexity, on the right side, for almost eight years.

January 29, 2000

Letter to editor, *Gloucester Daily Times*

It's Parties That Get Things Done

The January 18 issue of the [Gloucester Daily] *Times* reported the Audubon Society's rating of Cape Ann state legislators on conservation issues: Bruce Tarr (Republican), 57%; Brad Hill (Republican), 45%; and Tony Verga (Democrat), 73%.

Verga's percentage is lower than usual, but for the most part this is a typical political pattern. You don't have to [agree] with Audubon in the particulars to realize that these relative ratings roughly average out with those reported by other organizations on the voting records of even moderate Republican and mainstream Democratic legislators.

Similar party patterns are to be found for almost all other legislative voting issues in reports by both partisan and nonpartisan public interest organizations and foundations on either side of the political center. Each party stands pretty consistently on one side or the other of such different issues as campaign finance reform, tax equity, public health care, civil rights, executive branch confirmations, and (above all) judicial appointments.

All members of legislative bodies belong to one team or another. Of course no team always speaks with the same voice. There are usually a few players grumbling about this or that, but on almost all the plays they do what's expected of them. No politician can be against his own team on more than a few votes – especially when ambitious for a position of leadership within the party.

For example, Bruce Tarr is such a fine person and such an exceptional Republican that he is attractive to many local voters as practically an independent. But on the whole he votes with his party, and on the whole he always will. Otherwise he wouldn't be a Republican; he wouldn't be supporting other Republicans in state and national politics.

Fair enough. John Tierney does likewise with his Democratic Party. If these two were to run against each other, your vote would be for your candidate's party, like it or not, because he would vote in Congress for almost everything his party stands for.

Parties are made up of likeminded people. It all started with Jefferson and Hamilton. And it's parties that get things done, or prevents them from being done.

I would expect any Republican to agree with this truism, which many voters (especially "Independents") overlook. If you don't pay attention to party philosophy you often defeat your own purpose as far as overall results are concerned, all the way up to national and world affairs.

In one respect, however, the parties are not like football teams. They aren't playing for the same goals.

February 1, 2000
To Richard Altobelli

The Base of My Politics

Please locate p. 82 of the 1-24-00 *New Yorker*. It lays out the base of my politics, from 1936 onward. It's just a review, but someday I'll get the book itself. It's something that every journalist and pundit should absorb, and dear Mr McCain also (the only running Republican who might be open to it).

How's your gimpy leg?

February 2, 2000
To Gene Bailey

"A Necessary Evil"

This is a local letter to the paper but I thought I'd send it to you after reading your email on the Primary results. As for the candidates that you're cool about (esp Gore), all I can say is that I'm not un-enthusiastic because they're necessarily operating in an octave that's determined by our whole anti-intellectual and culturally degraded society. The criticism deserved in a higher octave is futile in any American political campaign! So my partisanship is often enthusiastic.

Did you read the review (in the *New Yorker*) of Garry Wills's brilliant book "A Necessary Evil"? It should be digested by all Democratic politicians and journalists as absolutely basic – almost as basic as religion!

February 4, 2000
To Gene Bailey

Step-by-Step Compromises

New parties or old parties, two parties or three, but what I argue is that an "independent" vote is feckless if it's not consonant in most respects with likeminded voters. You have to reform some party if you want to reform the country.

If you add up all the Democratic proposals that have been blocked by Republicans and then imagine they'd been passed, I think you'd feel a little more kindly about the one I put my meliorative hopes in.

As for objectives, of course I agree with you. But we have to climb out of the cultural octave we're in, with the company we have! Yes, that takes step-by-step compromises – provided the net motion is always upward. Wouldn't FDR agree?

What does Shirley think anent this family debate?

February 8, 2000

Letter to editor, *Gloucester Daily Times*

Importance of Any Politician's Party Affiliation

This is to emphasize the meaning of my letter to the editor printed on Thursday, Feb. 3, regarding the importance of parties in our politics.

The assigned headline read: "It's simply party politics as usual." To anyone glancing at the page, this caption was misleading. It implies a very common criticism of the way our state and federal system works.

On the contrary, the letter itself argues for the importance of any politician's party affiliation in the election process.

Old party, new party, reform party or fourth party – the badge is an essential political characteristic of the person up for a partisan election.

A voter may be registered as independent, or switch party sides any number of times, but the individual candidate supports a team of generally consistent value judgments, by which any party is inspired or empowered.

There is nothing inherently disgraceful about meaningful party politics. Democratic government can't work without it.

February 11, 2000

To Gene Bailey

If Unions Are Prohibited

Glasses case not mine. I was never there with a Peter. Which one, anyway?

I had a hunch that Shirley would be on my side – imperfect progress (or imperfect prevention of retrogress)!

I'm afraid McCain will sweep the election if he's nominated. My hope is that he will show up Bush before losing to him at their Convention.

The guy is all too persuasive. I was amazed to see him say on C-Span (in S.C.) that if unions are prohibited from contributing money without individuals' consent, corporations should be likewise prohibited to do so without STOCKHOLDERS' consent! For years I've been waiting for Democrats and pundits to riposte(sp?) with that cry!

I'm afraid that McCain's basic "conservatism" would be overlooked until it's too late to save the Supreme Court. His Party would not let him re-think any of his inherited political attitudes except those that he's chosen to point out.

… Have you oiled up your lawnmower?

February 25, 2000

To Gene Bailey

Ingrained (Quasi-Legal) Corruption

I had let my *Harper*'s subscription lapse because I don't like Lapham (the editor), but this article on the Shrub is worth a year of political scholarship! I'm very grateful to you for sending me it.

I hope the Democratic staff people will keep it pinned to the wall during the final campaign (if Bush wins the nomination). It's the best thing on ingrained (quasi-legal) corruption I've seen for many many years. Deep, detailed, ironically temperate.

But only a crash or recession – losses in all those portfolios – will bring the perfidy to general public attention. Who's going to be left holding the bag when all those securities deflate? To avoid personal "failure" they'd better unload on gullible little guys right now! Then the voters may take thought about Republican morality.

Thanks!

June 22, 2000
To Richard Altobelli

My Most Personally Beloved Politician

Ref: your letter 6-18-00:

Why not send a set of three to each of the two great libraries?

Don't worry about any duplication. They can always use extra copies and we can be sure that those institutions offer the best hope of preservation even unto posterity.

I was happy to see that you got an order for your gem. Have you donated one to the BPL?

I stand corrected about Adlai because I never read one of his books – as far as I can remember only small newspaper things. I now adopt your opinion about my most personally beloved politician (who did not remain a Democrat by accident).

I shall say nothing about the influence of a Democratic governor on the NH psyche.

October 22, 2000

Letter to editor, *Gloucester Daily Times, Boston Globe, New York Times*

Who Needs Political Parties?

National parties are groups of politically like-minded voters, active or passive. Though bound by certain rules of procedure, they are not like football teams competing for the same goals. They are more like social clubs, open to anyone as member or observer, with no secrets about what makes them for the most part like-minded. They are – or should be – recognized for what they agree on.

Most of the political values of each of its declared members are – or should be – understood by virtue of their identification with a party. Above all, those they nominate for office, are expected to act as much as possible according to those values.

In our culture of mass communication, dominated by commercialized TV, there is little room for extensive discussion of the easily confused complexities that make modern industrial society feasible. Individual politicians, whatever their personal motives or personalities, can neither get elected nor accomplish anything in office without the collective support of the party with which they are identified.

Conversely, therefore, a vote for an individual is a vote for a party. Every voter may well ask "WHY is So-and-So running on this ticket"? Almost always the answer to that question will indicate more about the actual effects of a candidate's past or future performance than any claims or promises, however sincere or insincere they may be.

It is sometimes very difficult for a voter to judge an incumbent even by the record of legislative votes or executive vetoes because the procedures of representative government typically involve separate decisions about intricate amendments to proposed bills already written.

For example, a YES vote may sometimes be used to kill a law or budget by tacking onto it something known to be beyond possibility of compromise for the majority – and vice versa for a NO vote or a presidential veto. Thousands of such decisions must be made every year in Boston and Washington. Even more important, a proposed bill or appropriation itself may be hundreds of pages long and full of lawyerly clauses with triple negatives or inconsistent details.

Votes are often taken before legislators have time to study the "language" they are asked to accept or reject. To vote a measure up or down they must then rely on party specialists or leaders to cast votes in accordance with their own general wishes.

If it is difficult for individual politicians to understand everything happening in their chamber, think how much more difficult it is for an individual going to the polls who hasn't even had time to follow the daily news beyond its headlines, or who has been able to take particular [interest] only in one or two particular issues!

Even executive orders (or cancellations) by a president or governor, sometimes crucially important to the regulation (or deregulation) of environment, public health, commerce, or the like, are often too technical or boring to capture the attention of competitive news-producers.

So a voter who ignores party labels has to do a lot of sheer guessing about what effect a particular candidate (no matter how attractive as a person) would actually have on state, country, or world if elected.

As a practical matter, the past and present pattern of a party's positions is at least as important as the personal qualifications of its individual nominee. It's the best quick clue to candidates' responses to future political pressures.

It's therefore the best means for a citizen to keep from casting a vote that cancels itself by indirectly supporting both sides of the same issues (which is what Independents often do, a major cause of political "gridlock").

If you can't read up on all the arguments like a scholar or a full-time pundit – all the biographies, all the records, all the executive orders and appointments, all the promises, all the detailed arguments – an overview is possible if you give credence to the collective positions taken by each candidate's club, year in and year out.

What does Party X or Y really CARE about? What seems to be the personal motives of those who belong to it? What has it done to STOP what you are opposed to? It is equally important to consider what a party has WANTED to do but failed for lack of legislative majorities.

In almost all cases the person elected will vote by party line. No one stands alone, even the president. In some particular instances you may be disappointed in your party, or in an elected member of it (as if in a member of your own family); but exceptions do not disprove the worth of reliable affiliation.

The only reason it seems to many voters that there's not much difference between our two major parties is the process of representative government itself. They must come to compromise at the stage of final agreement on legislation. It's the final version that gets into the news, not the initial positions on each side.

The adopted bill usually does not fully express the wishes of either party. The same voices that complain about a lack of distinction between the parties also cry out against the final "bickering" that may reflect deep differences about the initial draft of a proposal. The occasional gridlock they deplore comes about for the very reason that the differences are so pronounced.

The only way to alleviate such legislative impasse is to elect presidents and congressional majorities of the same party. Then things will start to move – either for better or for worse, according to your own public values.

The current campaign and presidential debates are deplorably narrow in political scope owing to the prevalence of commercial television and the practically unconstrained influence of money. It's too bad our political battles must be fought on a low intellectual level, with more appeals to self-interest at both ends of the economic spectrum than to the common good.

But such is the present reality. The American public will not even nominate a president who doesn't conduct a campaign according to the market. Just as every step in a computer program is based exclusively upon the present state of its system, which bears no trace of its past states or of external conditions, elections are conducted under day by day conditions of public opinion.

But performance in office, after election, is just as likely to be at a higher level than the campaign as it is to be at a lower. Thus it is that most nonpartisan voters, isolating their choice of an individual candidate from the political context, must start from scratch like amateur psychologists in their judgment of possible presidents, and do so on the basis of a very narrow band of evidence.

Political and economic conditions are infinitely richer and more complex than any philosophical or computer system. Our self-government could not function without the practical institution of parties. They organize, manage, and clarify the real-world muddle of conflicting and variable interests.

Without parties there would be no stable cooperation among groups and no continuity over time – as the founding fathers soon discovered after beginning with a rather theoretical philosophy of individualism.

So the presidential TV debates (which allowed no time for extended exposition or sequential argument) are best appreciated only when related to unmentioned party backgrounds. The words spoken by Gore and Bush make much more sense if you realize the base upon which [they] stand. Regardless of momentary issues and personalities, from Roosevelt vs Hoover and Truman vs Dewey to Clinton vs Dole, the same essential party differences underlie both motives and subsequent performance.

[Of course I speak as a partisan when I boil it all down to an unending battle for and against progressive society, both national and international. It's not hard to guess a full range of my political opinions!]

October 26, 2000

To Margaret Green

Nader May Make the Difference

I hear that things are very close in FL, and that Nader may make the difference. Please forward this to any Greens you may know! It appeared in the *Gloucester Daily Times*. It was written by Mr Brackett.

Next I'll forward one written by me.

We'll have to celebrate or commiserate this summer.

November 16, 2000

To Robert Akeret

Psychological Insight on the Part of Voters

Thanks for your notices of success. You anticipated a lot of movement when you wrote about personal memoirs; maybe this one on pictures will do the same.

Your work brings to mind the question of psychological insight on the part of voters. Again and again it strikes me at election time that most people seem unable to see past the superficials (as determined by PR agents or half-educated journalists) with empathy or at least sympathy combined with reason. I think almost all wrongheadedness in people of goodwill is a matter of narrow scope in both time and space – i e , their small "system" ignores the larger systems of which it is a part. One example of that is all the talk about education – only one side of the equation – with no mention of anti-education (=advertising), which is in direct opposition to critical thinking. Do you do any writing on these extensions of "pictures"?

I still hope when I'm next in NYC to talk over with you a note I've kept of some things Dora told me about the Peters family many years ago when we were driving across the country.

By the way, when I was in Switzerland last summer I saw a building sign AKERET from the train window somewhere between Zurich and Winterthur (where I spent a few days). It may have been a pharmaceutical firm of some sort, but that's almost a guess. Did your father come from that part of the country?

My best to Ann.

November 16, 2000

Letter to editor, *Gloucester Daily Times*

Electoral Weight

This unfinished election has illustrated two basic principles that have always been in healthy conflict with each other, even when confused or overlooked. One is the principle of states' rights (including local rights within states), a kind of typically American individualism. The other is the Federalist principle of the common good (especially in the form of national majority rule), also known as "Big Government".

As Bob Whynot has recently reminded us, there were good reasons for the Electoral College as the country was about to make the very contentious transition from the Articles of Confederation to the Constitution. Some of those reasons still apply, but in the modern world arguments against it have grown much stronger.

It will be at least eight years (if at all) before any constitutional amendment can be ratified. But there will be a much better prospect of reform, whereby the national popular vote is strengthened, if it entails compromise between the two principles rather than outright abolition.

Each state's electoral weight is now determined by its number of Congressional Representatives plus its two senators. If the senators were NOT counted each state would have a number of Electors directly proportional to its population. Small states would not remain more influential than their weight of population but they would still have a block vote (unless they split it up according to their own formula). Their state's right would be preserved.

In this election Gore would have had about 40 less electoral votes and Bush would have had about 60 less votes. Thus, to go along with his popular vote advantage of about 200,000, Gore would have gained a 20-vote advantage in the electoral votes. There would have been little or no dispute about the outcome.

This reform of course would not settle the 200-year-old competition between the idea of states' rights and the Federalist idea of "big government", which this election proves we need more of. There are no national criteria or guidelines for electoral procedures. If "big government" can protect consumers with food labeling rules, for example, why shouldn't it protect voters from the present unnecessary confusion? Even WITHIN Florida its own state government has been far too little.

The troubles we now witness could have been prevented with standardization of administrative procedure, which would threaten no one's individual rights or property. The autonomy of Florida counties has fostered managerial incompetence and conflicting laws that force disputes into the courts.

Twenty years ago the Grocery Manufacturers of America, fiercely competitive with each other, got together to devise standardized product codes (as well as shipping pallets) that eventually made possible the highly successful automated supermarket check-out. Surely the states of the nation (and the counties of the states) could get together, as the Federal government, to modernize our national elections.

I believe that even our present states-rights-prevailing Supreme Court wouldn't object to that. A lot of far more controversial measures have been getting by under the "Commerce Clause" of the Constitution.

A third topic has been brought to the fore by this election: the naive acceptance of data processing as infallible, coupled with the prevalent excuse for any error as a computer "glitch" or "software bug", when almost always the trouble is caused by careless human input. Mechanical systems themselves vary from A to Z in suitability of application.

Much of the Florida problem is even more basic: the design of forms! Have you ever noticed how cleverly your credit card bills encourage you to make partial payments (at high interest) rather than the full balance (at no interest)? Ballots should encourage you to act in your own interest!

November 16, 2000

To Rose Adamek

Election Will Make a Great Negative Difference

What a pleasure to hear from you – typed and all! I don't know what went wrong with our correspondence if it wasn't that my last letter to you went astray (6 Dec 99), or perhaps your reply (which I didn't get). Thanks for summarizing the steps of semi-hiatus. Anyway, now we're in tune.

I did go to Cyprus, Rhodes, Munich, Linz, Mainz, Rhine boat, Aachen, Metz, Nancy, ... , Turin, Sardinia, Milan, and Basel et al in Switzerland late last summer, but I'm planning on UK and Scandinavia, mainly for two weeks at a writers' hostel on Gotland (first half of Sept 00). So I would like to call on you, perhaps in late September. (I want to see Shandy Hall and the eastern counties and maybe the Channel Islands before coming home.)

I'm glad you're settled in a rose-covered cottage rather than wearing yourself out trying to teach the unwashed young something about our language. What are you reading these days? I don't know about Don Bosco (though the name rings: a book or a writer?) or the Salesians (a RC order?). I think we have a lot to talk about.

Yes, this election will make a great negative difference, perhaps not as much to us as to the world (viz., environment, UN affairs, peacemaking! "nationbuilding", disarmament). You perhaps have no idea how negative the Republicans (i.e., Protesticans) are about the common good, which they scarcely consider. It's too bad that the election campaigns must needs be waged in terms of a debased culture. There are endless arguments about education and no word at all about the anti-education (advertising) that cancels it out. And we remain the most individualistic citizens in the world. I recently saw Tony Blair giving a long televised speech to some American jurists – at a level of educated eloquence that no American politician can afford to try to match. We may not have fallen yet but we're certainly in decline, and all the Democrats (Catholicrats) can do is fight it (publically) on the TV level of culture. So the campaign differences are much much deeper than the half-educated journalists can see.

You see, I wear my heart on my sleeve!

December 13, 2000
To Manfred Hegemann

The Folly of His Naderism

Now Mr Moore may see at last the folly of his Naderism. Will he and his friends ever learn that politics is not merely Simon-pure political philosophy? Ten percent of Nader's Florida votes would have prevented this disaster.

Think of it: all 93 of the Federal Attorneys who prosecute the law will be Republicans. For at least two years (until House Democrats have the power to investigate things, and the Senate Democrats too) we'll have to rest our hopes at the grassroots – Jesse J., investigative journalism, and popular demonstrations.

... Has B finished the Klemperer second book yet? (It illustrates some of what you say. It appears that it's the damn Settlements that's at the center of present West Bank turmoil. I've been trying to remember the name of the PM who allowed them, much to my dismay, about 8 (?) years ago, probably the worst unnecessary decision in modern Israeli history, it seems to me. We are living through the Last Testament, which was started by the priestcraft of the Old.

January 1, 2001
To Gene Bailey

Loyalty to Clinton-Gore

It does my heart good to know your attitude! I'm hoping for the utmost partisanship. I just hope the Democrats will show a little loyalty to Clinton-Gore. For me the Party is like family: you don't abandon a hardworking relative who has shared your blood just because of mistakes or failures in public relations.

January 19, 2001
To Celia Eldridge

Ashcroft Is Worse

I find from C-Span that Ashcroft is worse than I'd thought. His bland "integrity" is devious, treacherous, and Byzantine even by Republican standards, like other sweet-talking Confederates in the Senate. Urge our boys to filibuster this until nobody in the country can forget what he did to Judge White in order to win his own election.

January 29, 2001

To Manfred Hegemann

Postbellum Sweet-talk with Stiletto Up the Sleeve

Good letter to Jeffords!

What I most have against Ash is his dirty hypocritical "integrity". He torpedoed Judge White in Republican caucus while giving White to believe that he supported him. It's the typically Confederate honor and morality that outrages me – postbellum sweet-talk with stiletto up the sleeve.

... I'm afraid Bush is going to be popular, especially if he gets away with this confirmation.

February 2, 2001

Letter to editor, *Boston Globe*

The South is Rising in D C

Derrick Jackson is no mere alarmist about Bush, Ashcroft, Rehnquist, and their ilk. The Republicans and the neo-Confederates have merged.

After the Civil War the Southern establishment learned to accommodate the national polity with sweet-talking pretenses of enlightenment, just as Republicans have learned to accommodate by gesture and rhetoric the demands of a social democracy.

Those joined forces, representing a national minority, always win power by means of gesture and rhetoric, at which they have both had to be more adept and disingenuous than genuine Democrats. Over the years, kicking and screaming, they have adapted themselves to black colleagues and such horrors as Social Security, but their basic values have changed very little in essence.

They love "states rights" because the more local their power the more they have their way, like the English barons who fought the people's kings. Much of their "honor" and "integrity" is that of Medieval barons wearing velvet gloves.

As the recent election showed, we now have the realization of Nixon's "Southern strategy".

February 18, 2001

To Manfred Hegemann

Larger Immoralities of Money and Power

No, you don't have it all wrong – possibly just some aspect of it. Is his own account of the Rich pardon in today's *Times* both the first and the last term in the other side of the equation? I can't explain it psychologically without knowing the guy personally but that part of your analysis is plausible.

To me the moral selectivity of public opinion nearly offsets in the equation his insensitivity to the "accepted behavior" you speak of.

Republicans (and most Americans) are morally insensitive to the much larger immoralities of money and power that are considered normal by the rich and powerful who seldom have to expose their private deals (e g , George W himself). And as for pardons, the Nixon and Iran-Contra cases are infinitely more outrageous.

So Clinton may have feet of clay but at least his integrity above the ankles puts most of his critics to shame. As I may have said to you before, he's like a Shakespearean hero with startling faults.

The inside Bush gang may be a little leery of opening debates about pardons. Or about Whitehouse gifts, lest Democrats start up some Congressional investigations. (They don't seem to have to worry about the journalists.)

Anyway, Clinton isn't rich and has never been as acquisitive as his enemies, any one of whom is scarcely tempted by any need for furniture and nicknacks. I think I'm with you there. I'm reminded of those suddenly famous black football stars who naturally don't know how to deal with luxury.

Gore may not be a great campaigner but I don't think he has feet of clay.

March 9, 2001
To Richard Altobelli

The Plutocratic Party

Thanks for the paper. It will be returned on or before our next rendezvous. I've read half of it already. It's tantalizing – whets my appetite for a straightforward biography – but a little too full of insider jargon for a common reader like me. Even allowing for a foreign language, the author is not a writer. But maybe the second half will be clearer and better organized. I know Frederick Lane, and this man is no Fred Lane!

Re: your letter of 2-0-01: If my Party is the "Imperial" one, what do you call Bush's? The Plutocratic Party?

Or the Moral Individualists? Or just Economic Totalitarians?

Or simply the Dominating Isolationists? What do you think of their Sec of Treasury? He's turning out to be the most shameless baron of them all.

I am very disturbed to hear about your heart trouble. "In and out of the hospital" sounds pretty serious from a man who never complains about personal things. I hope NASDAQ doesn't have anything to do with your train of winter setbacks.

I certainly won't ask you to load books anymore. Sometime this spring I'll find a way to pick up a load at your house. But I also want to see the beaver village at that time of year, plus a horse or two.

March 16, 2001
To George Hochfield

Looking for New Democratic Hero

The recent NYT article makes the BRT sound quite interesting. Do you know anyone connected with it? I'd like to get the name and address of the "dramaturge" or "artistic director" or whatever they call the script-selector, because I've got something that might be of interest to a Berkeley audience.

...

I shouldn't be surprised but I am, to read about the pop growth of CA since I lived there and thought it was quite enough. You are lucky to live in a pueblo that looks down upon the teeming throng of energy-vandalizing bottomlanders. I remember when you and the gang called me a "pioneer-in-reverse" for leaving it all.

Is Gray a good governor?

I'm looking for a new Democratic hero if Gore doesn't come to the fore at an appropriate time. Unless of course Ralph still can prove that there's no difference between the parties.

March 30, 2001

To Cynthia Fisk

Spiritual Selfishness

Sun the 8th sounds good. I'll call ahead.

If you've ever read some of Pat Robertson's dogmatically aggressive statements about Catholics, Episcopalians, and other "main stream" denominations (as anti-Christian, evil, etc) don't you wonder why none of them ever challenge the spiritual selfishness of his ilk? If religion were just a matter of saving individual souls (and hating the competition) I'd recommend compulsory atheism!

Emil Durkheim ["the father of sociology"], *The Elementary Forms of the Religious Life* – that's the book I was trying to remember when I spoke of the social basis of proper religion. Theology should start at that level and work its way up to "spirituality" – without skipping the intellectual element on the way. You're probably already at the top; I'm satisfied to be half way!

April 21, 2001

Letter to editor, *American Prospect*

New and Old Democrats

The parallel discussion between New and Old Democrats has been useful and stimulating. There is no need for bitterness or recrimination. Both sides are persuasive. Thesis and antithesis will come to synthesis if we raise them to the more philosophical level of persuasion that our Party has been neglecting. As far as political tactics are concerned we indeed need what Molyneux calls a "compelling critique" of the Republicans. But when we are publicly arguing the Democratic cause we also need a simply expressed criterion by which anyone may judge our own political propositions. What we require is a single ultimate test by which all Democrats can be distinguished from Republicans, regardless of our tactical or programmatic differences as means to that end.

Such a simple compendious criterion is the Common Good. This concept is implicitly the purpose of all Democratic proposals but (especially among Old Democrats) it is left unsaid. It should be made obvious, for example, that the welfare of the "working class" of the population is essential to the nation's or the world's common good. By the same token, as New Democrats emphasize, the welfare of the society as a whole requires efficiency of both government and economy. Obviously there is plenty of room for reasonable argument about whether or not certain policies (such as "free trade") can or do contribute to the common good, but by keeping the end in view we have a framework for discussion. Sometimes it is easy to test a political idea against this criterion of the common good (as in the case of G W Bush's proposed tax-cut), and sometimes it is not easy (as in the case of such complex technical issues as trade), but always the first question for clarification should be "How does it affect the COMMON good?"

That's the question with which we should confront every Republican claim and justify every Democratic effort (especially in environmental matters, for which we benefit from the support of many rich people who have asked themselves this very question). Of course our political rhetoricians may find a better term than the Common Good, but it should be one we can sew on all our banners. It should be our motto for teaching voters how to read Republican lips.

June 2, 2001
To Peter Anastas

Big Play for the Catholic Vote

Thanks for sending that intelligent review of Ben's books.

I've been hearing a lot about Roth lately – but I thought it was Philip Roth. Joseph sounds more interesting. (Henry, of course, is distinct in my mind.)

Republicans are making a big play for the Catholic vote (as Reagan did). That's what worries me most in politics now. In his Inaugural the young Bush referred to the Common Good (a term from Catholic theology) and no Democrat or columnist even noticed – the motto that rightly belongs to Democrats! Even before the abortion issue the Catholic hierarchy was Republican (vs. the priests and nuns), but now the partisan political philosophies seem irrevocably confused.

August 26, 2001
To Peter Anastas

Gore Deserves Sympathy Instead of Scorn

And Ralph Nader is still spouting selfrighteous defiance of Democrats for their impurity!

I think it's a disgrace the way so many liberals are blaming Gore for "losing" because he had no principles, and at the same time scorn him for losing Tennessee. He lost his own state because he opposed the tobacco forces and supported gun control, knowing full well how damaging that was to him with rednecks. Also I am disgusted that they have no sense of (deserved) loyalty. You'd think it was harder on them than it was on the poor guy himself!

Kerry is a good man, but unless he shows far more political flair (for people outside the Northeast) I don't see how he could carry the country. Al Gore already has! Anyway, Gore deserves sympathy instead of scorn; and gratitude. So I'm for Gore by more than default, at least until a better man shows himself (it being 4 years too soon for Hillary).

Bush is more of a shock than a surprise (given his campaign statements). Nader's effrontery (still!) is a sickening epitome of the immature personality. Cf Gore's concession speech.

December 15, 2001

To Manfred Hegemann

FDR and Clinton Always Understood

I am on edge but not off it yet.

I am not totally incapacitated but I am frustrated by living in such interesting times (and by so many wasted hours in newspaper reading, and by self-indulgence in travel) that my work-in-progress hasn't been progressive enough. Now come the obligations of Christmas and other decent diversions!

Were you in Germany too – or where and when? I had very interesting visits (after Sweden and Finland) to Berlin, Leipzig, Dresden, and Nuremburg (before St Malo, Guernsey, Norwich, and London), getting home on October 2. [I was in Gotland on 9-11.] There was no room for you and Brigitte on my plane, though I had hoped to save you seats.

You seem to have stereotyped my views about the Israeli, just because I try to display both sides of the differential equation, so I no longer try to disabuse you, since you are a perfect liberal (by my definition) in all domestic matters, and I know your values match mine at least approximately. But certainly Barak has taken shameful advantage of Bush's definition of our "war" to justify his own. The Israeli minority is as helpless as is ours at the moment.

What should have been called an international police action with military support has been defined and generally accepted as a military action supported by police. Anyway, I can't think of any statute that allows Bush to invoke martial law without a Congressional declaration of war. Such a declaration implies warpowers abhorred by business! Therefore we repeat the legal atrocity of Viet Nam et al. I think Bush has done more or less what a Democratic administration would have done in a military way, quite competently: it's the diplomatic and political arrogance of deified selfishness that dismays me. I certainly agree with you about all that.

I doubt that either Daschle or Kerry is electable to the presidency, given our money-powered process, but they're the kind we need. (Besides, they're both senators.) I'm still loyal to Gore, for lack of better alternative; but he'd better find an effective manner of coming out of the closet. Nobody in history has suffered such a wracking and important personal disappointment, yet he's castigated for his stalwart behavior (despite having been castigated for over-aggressiveness in debates!).

I am really disgusted at the way many liberals are turning on him for largely selfcontradictory reasons. Most of their pundits don't understand that dealing with Republicans is and always has been the first and foremost political problem – not loudly proposing policies that for the most part liberals take for granted as the ultimate objective for their party of the common good.

FDR and Clinton always understood ...

So: good to hear from you! MERRY CHRISTMAS and HAPPY NEW YEAR, especially to Brigitte!

PS: Clio still barks at me, confusing herself. She's still in love with Harto.

April 5, 2002
To Peter Anastas

Number One Political Task

About Bush, yes indeed. I have never felt so keenly the decadence of the USA. E.g., when unions desert the liberals as soon as the present or future common good is said to threaten their jobs. I'm afraid that most Americans are simply selfish (though of course the "selfishness" of labor is much closer to the common good than the selfishness of the rich). But there is still an essential difference between Republicans who vote for their own good and those Democrats who vote disinterestedly for social welfare and environment. Ever since TR the number one political task is to defeat Republicans, as Clinton understood. Only then, he knew, would good causes have more than a compromised chance. If the Cans take both houses of Congress this year nothing will stop the degradation of the democratic dogma and the nationalistic brand of patriotism.

I'm only saying that I probably agree with you about everything!
...

September 6, 2002
To Manfred Hegemann

In Greater Political Danger

It's good to hear you're still alert and kicking. We'll be 76 any day now.

I'm sure you have more than a few other thoughts, but those are grist enough for the moment.

Clio attacked and mortally wounded a greyhound walking by her house on a leash. Emergency surgery at the vet's was unsuccessful.

Owner (who'd rescued her dog from the racing industry) was naturally devastated. Because Clio had been showing no sign of behavioral improvement – despite all the wonderful joys of her life – Cathy, after paying damages and sympathizing entirely with the owner – reluctantly and tearfully and bravely decided that there was too much danger of future attacks, perhaps even against children – decided that she had to take Clio in for her last ride a couple of days later. You can imagine her grief, and Michael's, and mine.

... I wonder if you father could have known of Albert Speer. I've been reading a lot about Berlin too, as it appears in various books (like Shirer's excellent one, and Wouk's). Next time I see you I'd like to see the history of Berlin you mentioned.

I was very impressed with what I saw there last year (soon after 9-11). It's sadly ironic that there was a spontaneous public display of flowers of sympathy for us in Berlin, reflecting a cordial attitude expressed toward Americans, who now seem about to betray their alliance in international moral progress. I admire Schroder for speaking up against Bush.

I would support a war against Irak if the UN and/or NATO and/or the EU approved of it. I'm afraid Bush is going to do a PR blitz to bulldoze it through Congress. (But at least the Demos are making him go to that trouble. John Kerry is taking a lead.) Bush is timing his blitz to dominate domestic matters during the election campaign. We're in greater political danger than almost ever before.

I urge you to read WINDS OF WAR and its sequel. Very interesting, informative, and exciting reading – much better and more sustained for mental recreation than a mystery story!

These are my selected thoughts.

October 13, 2002

To Peter Anastas

Only Bulwark against Bush

Thanks for the good advice.

Give Daschle credit for quietly turning Bush a long way from his first demands and at the same time cutting our losses before it's still not too late to wake people up about what in the long run is most important of all, namely defense of the senate (via economic issues), the WORLD's only bulwark against Bush. That lost cause is not yet entirely lost, but it would have been without his pragmatic tactics. We all float on the sea of American sub-intellectual culture, so this is the price of misguided democracy.

The best speech of all was Gore's, about two weeks ago in SF, which I happened to see on C-Span.

October 18, 2002

To Peter Anastas

I Fear Trent Lott

Thanks. My article was timely (the second time around) because I had taken your advice and called Muench (sp?). As you thought, everything was piling up on him and as we talked he pulled it out. So at least I got a word in immediately after the reproachable article about lack of response to the Charter affair.

He seems like a nice intelligent guy. One of these days I'll leave a few of the petition sheets in your box for your casual use.

Yes, by all means, I'll be at the DT Bookstore, and the reading too. I congratulate you on an elegant retirement schedule!

Now that you mention it, I have seen Demo (only) signs uprooted. Could it be that the vandals who uproot official street signs all year round are Republicans?

Step by step Bush has gotten the masses so immersed in military thinking that by election day they'll be persuaded it's too late for any alternative to his kind of "leadership". The Korea scare just strengthens his hand in every direction. I fear Trent Lott (as next Majority Leader) as much as Bush himself, seeing that the House and Supreme Court need only the Senate to complete the Degradation of the Democratic Dogma with authoritarian sophistry?

October 28, 2002
To friends

City Charter Commission

I have been advised that not all Gloucester voters read the GDT editorial page in every issue! Therefore I am repeating below a My View column that I submitted on Sept 25, 2002, but that was not printed until October 17, about three weeks later, long after my immediate response to a news article about the Charter. So in case you missed it please read below, and perhaps forward this message to any Gloucester voter you might think interested. It concerns a very rare opportunity for participation in non-partisan politics – or at least for a rare understanding how the City of Gloucester actually works.

CITY CHARTER REVIEW BRINGS OPPORTUNITIES

Gloucester is very fortunate to have elected an open-minded mayor who immediately called for professional examination of the city government's organization and practices. (I refer to the [Gloucester Daily] *Times* story of Tuesday, September 24.) We are even more indebted to him, the City Council, and the City Clerk for having already started the process by which citizens can petition for a public review and possible revision of the city Charter.

The Charter is our local constitution, which we adopted by a similar process over twenty-five years ago. When Gloucester progressed from the "Plan E" form of municipal government to our present "Home Rule" charter it was like the national replacement of the Articles of Confederation (1781) with the US Constitution (1789). Bear in mind that the Constitution was legally created and adopted by the people of the separate States, not by the previous Congress of the Confederation.

But even the final Constitution, by its own provisions, recognized the possible need for future Amendments. The first of many, almost immediately, were those known collectively as the Bill of Rights – additions rather than mere corrections, as were many of those that followed. Others, later, were basic changes. So also we voters, as well as the mayor and council, now have the opportunity for a "Constitutional Convention" – by means of an elected Charter Commission. Such a body, after detailed study and open hearings, may either recommend no change at all or draft a revised charter for approval or rejection by the city's voters.

(It's even possible for the Commission to propose an entirely different type of municipal government, as defined by Massachusetts law. But I doubt that such a radical change would attract significant support, seeing that the present charter has been well tested and is generally regarded as a definite improvement over the past experiment with Plan E.)

There are certain essential requirements and guidelines under Massachusetts law. First and foremost, at least fifteen percent of the registered voters (probably about 3000) must sign the petition to put the question of creating a Charter Commission on the ballot in 2003. Bob Whynot, the City Clerk, is the very helpful administrator of the entire process. I do not yet know all the details. At his office the present charter is available for inspection. You go there to get blank petition forms for circulation.

Thus voters must first petition for "Adoption or Revision of Charter or Suggestion of Charter Amendment". Your signature commits you to nothing but a wish to further the process of review, even if the outcome should be no change at all. In effect it signifies your approval of something like the proceedings in Philadelphia over two hundred years ago, which were hotly debated, almost gridlocked, but ultimately acceptable to all thirteen colonies.

There may not be thirteen factions in Gloucester but we certainly have a diversity of interests not necessarily in conflict with each other. Many of them are affected by the charter. For example, it seems to me that we don't always recognize that the separation of powers requires the separation of functions. I believe there are structural ways to prevent such financial fiascoes as the unauthorized cost overruns on the North Gloucester sewage project. I also believe that we could take useful advantage of a few generally overlooked Massachusetts statutes and Federal guidelines that govern municipal administration.

But there are many other perhaps more important questions for consideration, such as those regarding the mayor's powers of appointment, lengths of executive and legislative terms, the functions of voluntary boards or regulatory agencies, and dozens of others in the realm of community development. Few of the proposals are likely to be revolutionary in themselves, yet when incorporated as a self-consistent working document they may all contribute to clearer and more efficient selfgovernment.

But there is one important idea to emphasize. Again, a charter is a constitution: it is a framework for legislation, not a collection of ordinances or a statement of policies. For the most part it's a ratification of general principles according to which we make or alter our ordinances in the future – under continuously variable conditions of public opinion and Commonwealth or federal law. I suspect that our charter commission, if we succeed in getting ourselves one, will find that making this distinction will be a time-consuming part of its deliberations.

Gloucester's citizenry is amazingly rich in expert knowledge, talent, diversity of experience, creative leadership, and unselfish goodwill – all of which can be brought to bear and integrated if there are enough signatures on the petition to establish a charter commission. This kind of local democracy is not possible at higher levels of government. Gloucester could become a model for other small cities in the Commonwealth – and even provide some tips for one or two of the colonial towns hereabout.

November 7, 2002

To Manfred Hegemann

Deceived by Hope

I don't collect jokes, I just forward them.

I expected to be depressed on Wed morn but I had thought that at least O'Brien (gov MA) and Mondale would win. Maybe the jolt will do the Party some good in the long run, but in the meantime Bush is running the world with his storm-troopers, and he may be successful enough ex officio to enhance his power to the point of no return.

I've been reading a lot about Germany lately (right now Goebbels' *Diary*). Of course our Republicans are not Nazis and we still have social tolerance and liberty and a strong legal system, etc., but the parallels between Republican power-plays (especially in FLA 2000) and the National Socialists' are striking. I think especially of the Big Lie(s) technique.

For over two years I've been too distracted from my writing by the endless hopes and fears of public affairs (including the NE Patriots), so at least now in my political depression I can (mostly) let all my subscriptions lapse, minimize radio and TV, and try to forget social reality until a knight in shining armor turns up to revive my feckless hopes – and slow down my work-in-progress again! If Gore comes on as strong and wise as he was in his speech about a month ago I'll stick with him.

I'm going to visit in LA et al for a few weeks in January. Until then I'm scurrying to make the best of a hermit's chance to catch up a bit.

No dog, just a cat. I can't deal with further complications.

Cathy has been working night and day as the de facto leader of the Glo Demo City Committee, and has really done wonders with it – only to meet this disappointment. Imagine: a Mormon as our governor and another as Chm of the Senate Judicial Committee! It's hard to believe how gullible American voters are – even allowing for their selfishness.

My best to dear Brigitte.

November 8, 2002
To Catherine Bayliss

Residual Prejudice against Women in Power

I hope you have recovered threads of hope. I had expected to have a depressing Wed morning, but I was confident that at least we'd have the new governor. I think it's only residual prejudice against women in power that made her lose. Anyway, everybody appreciates what you've done to wake up the GDCC.

It looks bleak now, and is, but I think the pundits are overreacting. It's no worse than it was when Raygun won – at least from the domestic point of view. For two and a half years I've been telling people not to underestimate Bush as an intelligent salesman. The electoral balance is still close.

Are you supporting Phil Johnson? It doesn't seem fair to blame him, from what little I know.

I still don't understand why "soft money" was more evil than "hard money". Does it have something to do with a Sup Court ruling?

November 11, 2002
To Manfred Hegemann

The Big Lie

I've been thinking exactly the same thing about the Cans' mindsets. Think of their storm-troop tactics at Miami two years ago! And always the Big Lie driven in by repetition and by intimidating journalists.

Allowing for the differences in our political system and general history, the patterns (if not the degrees) are very similar.

But of course you can't say anything like that without being accused of calling them Nazis, because that's the level of our unanalytical journalism. (Apparently even in Germany – witness Haider's lady minister – who tries to draw a comparison with Bush on somewhat different grounds.) I would like to contribute ideas for your PhD thesis.

... I'm actually going to Southern CA to stay with my half-sister and look around, especially at the new museums. May get as far down as San Diego and as far up as SF.

... Wow! I'm VERY happy that you sent me the Garrison Keillor piece. He's my hero of American culture. I listen to him every Sat night from six to eight (during kitchen work), primarily for his wonderful boasts about being a liberal and very succinctly making fun of the Cans. His political humor really cheers me up. His parodies of Ventura are side-splitting, not to mention Bush. I have to turn down some of the music but the serious comedy skits and monologues are usually works of genius. But I've heard or seen by such grim attacks by him as you've sent. I'm very grateful. Where was it published? I'd love to see more of his political analysis.

... I didn't know you had a nephew. From which of your sisters?

December 14, 2002

To Torsten Kehler

Taking Advantage of Dixiecrat Emotions

Looking back:

This is a residue of the Civil War, the sub-text of "states rights". It still is, with people like Lott and Ashcroft. It is embarrassing to Republicans, who welcomed Lott when (as a Congressman) he switched parties, who as usual have been dragged kicking and screaming into lagging but socially progressive positions, and who on the whole have been taking advantage of Dixiecrat emotions ever since. There would have been no surprise or outcry about Lott's showing his heart on his sleeve if they hadn't been worried about losing electoral votes in the North.

The Democrats are not yet pure but they have gradually been purged of the Confederates since they were FDR's No.1 political problem.

Do you know that even civilized Europeans like Jos Conrad have been fooled by the phoney tradition of Confederate honor and aristocracy? In modern form Lott, Ashcroft, et al have learned the art of sweet-talking their management of black constituencies. "States rights" always suit the plutocracy, as they did the Medieval English barons, because it's much easier to keep local than national economic power. (Except in cases like the Florida 2000 election, when their judicial principle, like civil rights, goes by the board.)

December 15, 2002

To Victoria Bayliss Mattingly

Al Gore Has Just Dropped Out of 2004

... As you must know, the 'Cans are lamentably happy, with all three branches of gov't. They have already shown everyone that there *is* a difference between the two parties, aside from private morality. Al Gore has just dropped out of 2004, so we may get a good man from Massachusetts as our next nominee. I think he'll speak out to my way of thinking. ...

December 30, 2002

To Roger Fisk, Senator John Kerry's Office

General Philosophy for the Common Good

I was very glad to be in your audience when you addressed the Gloucester Democratic City Committee last summer, and I am now taking advantage of your invitation to communicate.

Please bring to the Senator's attention at least the last two pages of the enclosed article from the *U.S. Naval Institute Proceedings* magazine of December 2002. I think it would give him some reserve ammunition against the Bush administration when they boast about their military successes and start attacking him.

I urge him to continue his own aggressive but circumspect attacks on Republican policies and hypocrisies, and continue to lead other Democratic candidates with his criticisms in military and foreign affairs (without of course abandoning the so-called traditional Democratic values). He should not try to change his "aristocratic image". Common people love aristocrats who fight for justice, especially when they're not afraid of hawks. Witness FDR and his New Deal!

I think Senator Kerry can win in 2004 if he emphasizes a general philosophy for the Common Good (or some term of the same meaning), whereby all other proposals and criticisms, in both foreign and domestic affairs, will be argued as for or against the benefit of society as a whole. That's what our recent Democrats have been failing to do. He is one man who can persuade voters that National Security, Social Welfare, Labor, Business, Environment, and Culture must give, take, or compromise as moral and economic parts of the commonwealth.

I suggest that every face-to-face debate start with the challenge "Why are you a Republican?" Make the opponent try to defend the record of his narrow-interest party. Then show how our party is at last stating its hitherto largely subconscious philosophy. Then all our particular "issues" make more sense to independent voters.

Can you get the Senator to read this letter?

February 19, 2003
To *Gloucester Daily Times* Op-Ed Page

War Only If and When Necessary

Civilization began in southern Irak – known to scholars as Sumer. Before the civilizations of Egypt, India, or China. That was when the Tigris and Euphrates rivers still emptied separately into the Persian Gulf. Agriculture began in Irak. The first cities formed in Irak. The first writing and numbering. The world's first accounting and the world's first literature. For better or for worse, the Tower of Babel.

The epic of Gilgamesh and the Bible both came out of Irak. In part we share them both with Muslim civilization.

It is true that Sadam Hussein's Irak is an anti-civilization. But it is an evil that should be dissolved and reformed by civilized means. That is to say, by war only if and when necessary.

But at present there are other anti-civilizations more urgently dangerous to world civilization, North Korea and Al Qaida, both of which have proved their immediate aggressiveness. Why are they comparatively soft-pedaled in our foreign policy? Why are they spared the fervor of our president's personal crusade?

Today's crisis seems to be a question of personal psychology. The private emotions or indirect economic motives of the one decision-maker are not irrelevant to the future of civilization, even if the proposals he chooses from are perfectly reasonable in the ideologies of those who compete for his approval.

Cataclysmic intercontinental nuclear missiles and internationally infectious terrorism should alarm anybody's civilization as much as does an evil dictator who could be further constrained at least a few more months by a combination of continued inspections and a continuous tightening of international monetary exchange between civilized and uncivilized dealers in military material or the transport thereof.

As we sincerely preach democracy we must allow for the world's democratic opinion about if and when actual events determine a just war. At least we should have a logical justification for arrogating to ourselves a morality superior to that of most Western theologians.

The United Nations – civilization's imperfect forum – has been an unprecedented advancement in human history – one of the greatest single achievements in a cultural evolution that began not far from the same marshlands and its age-old settlements that Sadam Hussein has savagely obliterated in his own country since the first Gulf War rightly won UN approval.

March 22, 2003

To draftgore@draftgore.com

Emphasize Gore's Proven Reputation

Please organize some sort of e-mail petition that you can deliver to Mr Gore, simply stating grassroots support – with unpublicised copies to his major erstwhile financial contributors.

Also start collecting big-name endorsements for well-timed release in 2004.

You need to draft a careful manifesto that can be sent to all local Democratic committees, as well as to journalists. I suggest that it be diplomatically addressed to include everyone who already has a favorite (as I have) among the present Democratic candidates, asking them to think of Gore as at least their second choices in the event that the present favorite does not make it through the semi-finals, especially if it appears that the Boston convention is not going to make an overwhelming choice otherwise.

Please emphasize Gore's proven reputation in ALL parts of the country, and at every level of sophistication.

Contrary to conventional wisdom, I think it is possible for him to excite the whole country (and dismay the Republicans) if he is genuinely drafted in default of the others. But it will require that his fans be on farsighted good terms with the present panel of primary candidates. Almost all of them would make good running mates or Cabinet officers on a desperately needed dream-team!

PS: I got your notice from the *American Prospect* magazine ad.

March 24, 2003
To Gene Bailey

Pounding Away at Bush's Economic Folly and Injustice

Yes. But it's imperative that Democrats concentrate on domestic politics from now on, rather than upon the war itself, which is a done deal and will take its course. They should avoid appearing to care more about protest than about the next election, which is the only real means to affect the course of future world events. Discreet Party politics is more important than ever, and every liberal utterance should have that in mind – practical, realistic politics that recognizes our liberal New England mentality as unrepresentative. We can hope to sway by reason and goodwill but we can't expect it. Only pounding away at Bush's economic folly and injustice can do the trick. That's why I think we should have a default plan for the next fifteen months. When the time comes it may be that Gore will look like the 800-lb gorilla on our side.

Happy springtime out there in the west!

March 25, 2003

To Richard Altobelli

Wartime Macho-Sentimentality

No, in Bahrain. There have been some anti-American demonstrations but at least they seem safe from the war itself.

By the way, do you know anything about Gen. Wesley Clark (Ret.) (who now appears on CNN)?

I wish the anti-war demonstrators here had more political commonsense, now that the war is a done deal. They just play into the hands of Bush's rabble-rousers (re: today's Krugman in NYT). The wartime macho-sentimentality will have to run its course before reason can be encouraged again.

How are you and yours?

March 27, 2003

To Richard Altobelli

Degradation of the Democratic Dogma

Re: Hersh in this week's *New Yorker*: compare the fake information that started the Spanish-American War!

Clark has been urged to file for Demo primaries. He was good in Yugo, I remember. Now a CNN commentator.

Might be good VP nominee???

Tony Blair most interesting character in the world.

Oh I do like Adams.

(Degradation of the Democratic Dogma may be what you have in mind. It's the best title for our present regime.)

... I'm very sorry about your domestic news.

April 25, 2003

To local Democrats

Why Sign Up as a Democrat? Thoughts for Recruiting

Not all Republicans are alike, but their votes all converge as one at the highest level. By the same token, not all progressives are alike. But when all their votes converge in the Democratic Party they can replace a regime in Washington that ignores our common good and defies the democracy of our allies.

In our national political system such convergence does not resemble the so-called grassroots process in which a single level of growth expresses the power. But it does resemble the life of a tree, where the roots converge to form a trunk of nourishing support for many branches of the body-politic, and a lofty diversity of economic and cultural interests.

If people of goodwill converge from their various roots of interest they can rise as an oak stronger and far more comprehensive than the pointed spruce tree of the Republicans that converges at the top. We can make a just society all the way up from the acorn to a wide spread of twigs and leaves.

But this purpose is defeated by those who vote for candidates exclusively on the strength of single issues or personal attractiveness. Every candidate is supported by a party, and every elected representative, at every level from local district to the presidency, whether or not agreeing with that party on every issue, is almost always going to act in support of that party. It's the party that wins or loses control of the all-important committees in Congress, as well the executive power that largely determines the judicial power. Your particular interests, even if they are not particularly supported by a majority of your own party voters, can be carried to fruition by that same party, simply on the strength of being your family. So it has happened for much of our civil rights and environmental legislation.

Every vote with a party rises all the way up the tree like sap for foliage. That's the reason to *vote* for Democrats in the primaries as well as in the final elections.

The reason to *register* as a Democrat is that you can directly participate in the selection and fertilization of the roots themselves. Even if you already vote Democratic without identifying yourself as one of us, and even if you never come to a Democratic meeting or contribute a nickel to the Party, your name added to the City Clerk's rolls as a member of our Party will express your political values by impressing other voters with the viability of decent party politics.

The size of our partisan registration can also warn Republicans to back off in their attacks upon the past accomplishments of our truly constructive party. Keep reminding yourself of the Supreme Court.

May 6, 2003

To George Hochfield

Party That Has Obstructed Justice

Our spring is worse than yours.

The nine, indeed, don't yet look promising. I wish they'd speak out, like James Carville. They should be criticizing Republicans in general (that whole damned party that has obstructed justice and fostered injustice for a century), as well as Bush2 in particular, who's turned out worse even than Reagan, on the basis of values. It's silly to argue with each other about particular policy instead of principle. Has anyone in debate ever asked "Why are you a Republican?"? Before Reagan they soft-pedaled their tribal identity. Will any Crat ever have the courage to attack the Cans' real motives?

(Not while our journalists – except Ms Dowd? – remain so blind to both personal and social psychology.) Our candidates are always too worried about defending or proposing this or that grove of trees.

So I'm still hoping the nine will neutralize each other and in a last-minute drama we can turn to Gore and/or Wesley Clark.

The latter has an astonishing brain and an ideal personality. It's too bad this newfangled primary craze stands in the way of good old-fashioned convention politics!

So it seems that I agree with you at least on strategy.

... I'd like to see more of Washington, but I won't make the effort until the Can spirit is exorcised in at least one branch of government. For you and M, though, have a good trip!

Did you get my message about Ralph?

May 29, 2003
To Jamie Cope

Some Abstract Thought

I'm glad you're in touch with the earth!

And thanks for approaching the Crat office. If it's moribund, don't be discouraged. It can come to life like a spring daffodil as people get more interested in the world's fate, including ours.

The Crat Party is really a coalition of groups and minds best defined as anti-Republicans, lacking only a stated philosophy that comprehends what's in common with them all – which is what I'm interested in proposing. What's missing in its welter of good policies and programs and proposals is some abstract thought about the COMMON GOOD!

The Republicans are all too good at promulgating their narrow philosophy of selfishness – mainly by concealing it!

... Somebody made a mistake down here: a single good day has burst through!

May 30, 2003
To Jamie Cope

Partisan Voting

I agree entirely. The only thing that can save us is a recession soon enough and long enough to awaken the American people from their TV opiates and make the effort to think critically – at least to the extent of partisan voting.

(I assume that's what you mean by an incipient tidal wave. But the tidal wave started by Raygun may be rolling in the other direction.)

The garden I attend is indoors and unseasonal, so my May is not as soothing as yours ...

June 8, 2003
To Mark Power

What If Maggie Were Still in Charge?

Blair may have been duped, to the shocking discredit of his personal intelligence, but I simply cannot believe that he knowingly lied in his statements. Anyway, he's still the only diplomatic link we have left to Western Civilization, and we're better off with him than without him. What if Maggie were still in charge?

I don't think I've ever been to Peterborough, but next time I'll verify your judgment. Durham has been my favorite cathedral, the earliest English Gothic, which I saw on my first trip to the UK. In later years I've avoided late Gothic (all over the Continent), looking everywhere for Norman or Romanesque beauty. In most places Gothic outlived its functional beauty, Ruskin to the contrary notwithstanding.

What the Anglicans (still at least schismatically catholic) have done to interiors is as nothing to what the real Protestants have done to them in northern Europe where Catholic exteriors remain!

(I always suffer a little jolt when I see or hear Episcopalians [Anglicans] referred to as Protestants, since we claim to be members of the "holy catholic and apostolic church" – which probably raises your hackles; but I can argue the factional reason for it when next we meet ... But there's no doubt that most Anglicans ARE as Protestants as the whole country is, including "conservative" Roman Catholics, who are as muddled in theological culture as the Protestant majority is.)

But I like your description of Seville, where I never had a chance to get inside the Cathedral.

Please volunteer your opinions at any time ... Thanks for promising to vote, as long as it's on the Democratic ticket.

Things have gotten so serious here – really ominous – that any non-Democratic vote is a vote for (Protestican) Republicans!

June 24, 2003

To friends and family

Gore and Clark

"The United States is a 225-year rolling revolution ... We are the embodiment of the Enlightenment ..."

Gen. Wesley Clark

It appears that the people of Moveon are Dean sympathizers (hence the timing of this vote). I have no objection to that. Only at the very last minute have they opened the vote to write-ins, but at least they have finally done so.

Still, they are doing a public service and I believe they are honest in their goodwill. But if Dean gets 50% of the straw vote, and their one-million-plus voter endorsement, it will prematurely tend to foreclose liberal support for other candidates. (As it is, only C-span watchers can have a real sense even of the official candidates. I find that many Democratic journalists are still missing the scope of our possibilities.)

It is hard for me to decide between Gore and Clark, but I will vote for Clark. He and Gore seem to be sympathizers with each other (as well as with Clinton). Clark is clearly the most attractive candidate for the full spectrum of voters, and I think has all the qualities, credentials, and values that a liberal patriot would want. I've seen and heard him at great length on C-Span and NPR.

Imagine an administration with both of them at the top! There'd be plenty of room for Dean and Kucinich in the cabinet (and Graham & Kerry too, if we can spare them in the Senate).

July 29, 2003

To Mark Power

Mistaking Bush as an Honorable Gentleman

Thanks for your conscientious follow-up. I like to hear from you, but I can get the *Guardian* web-page when I need crosschecking, though I find it too confusing in trying to get straight news instead of opinion columns – and then there's the *Independent* and all sorts of other masthead entities that I don't have to time to figure out – something like trying to understand the various shires and counties and ridings and districts and other institutions of UK geography!

But I'm still suspending my *moral* judgment of Blair, hoping that the Parliamentary committee (or judicial) inquiry will establish some facts (I saw Kelly during the inquiry at some length on C-Span. In any case I continue to admire TB's long-range motives (for the world); and his turpitude, if any worse than, say, FDR's, is insignificant compared to Bush's et al.; and his competence dwarfs anyone else on the scene. Moral or immoral, I still think his fundamental mistake, pragmatically speaking, was mistaking Bush as an honorable gentleman of the educated kind that Brits take for granted even when referring to known scoundrels!

With these provisos, if I'm wrong about Blair it will be the only serious political disillusionment of my life since I was disabused of

US "conservative" motives at the age of about ten. So who isn't a spin-doctor in any democracy once in a while? One has to be an equivocating relativist at times, or else give up keeping his eye on the prize, which is the common good! I don't think all power is bad per se, as long as it isn't selfish or cruel like that of Republicans. One thing I'm sure of: Blair is no Republican! (He may be a Clinton.)

... I miss your green and pleasant foster-land. Right now, reading a biog of Laurie Sterne, I'm immersed in East Yorkshire, but I thirst for the beer and scene everywhere from the Scillies to the Shetlands via Guernsey and Norwich. (I keep thinking of the horse we met at your pub.)

It will be bitterly ironic if the Brits bring down Blair and his party while we reelect Bush and his next year. If the converse happens there will be hope for the world.

July 30, 2003
To George Hochfield

As Unassailable as a Liberal Can Get

Ever since your last I've been mulling the word *transcendental*, which has always seemed elusive when applied generically. Metaphorically, I now gather, it can be used in an ontological (Kantian) sense as the field *within which* you experience everything, rather than (as I had thought) the general object *to which* all experience points. So I suppose (and always have) that the Emersonian meaning is the latter, sort of. So your message has been very useful to me as a common reader, and I thank you for it.

So sometime I'll take you up on your promise to explain Emerson. I turned away from him when I read his categorical rejection of *organized* religion, as if religion and culture in general are not *genetically* (before they transcend) social. It's that damned individualistic *over*-reaction to the old Catholicism that's still the bane of American society (notwithstanding the intellectual confusion of contemporary Catholic conservatives and progressive Protestants, with Jewish counterparts on both sides). God knows we're grateful to the Reformation for liberty, progress, and enlightenment: but why kick away the ritualistic foundations of society and government?

Anyway, that's why I'm a Democrat rather than a Republican (or worse yet, an "Independent").

And that's why I was pleased years ago when I read that Melville said something like "I don't coruscate in Emerson's rainbow." [Can you guide me back to that quote and correct it for me?]

But I agree, from what little I read many years ago, that E is a superb writer, and that Thoreau can be too boring, as in the *Week on* ... (even though I went to it in topographical interest). I liked the rowboat surveying in *Walden*, where we occasionally swam as a special treat when I was a kid and we had no car, but not much else.

I look forward to your anthology, because, as you can see, I need the education.

... Yes, we need a "real candidate". It isn't Dean. Kerry is real, but if he doesn't make it through the semifinals decisively I'm for the man below, an amazingly sympathetic person of great intellect and prestige, and about as unassailable as a liberal can get. At least on a ticket with Gore, who would surprise people this time around. If we can just win back the Washington platform we'll have opportunity to liberalize the country step by step, coopting the do-gooders, as Clinton started to do without a wish-list manifesto.

Indignation lacerates my breast whenever I encounter self-righteous purists who'd rather be right than win.

August 15, 2003
To George Hochfield

Tax Cuts for Rich People Have a Dual Purpose

I saw Davis for a few minutes on CNN last night. He seems intelligent, rational, and competent! (He may be nasty in campaigning, but he can't be any worse than the Can norm.) Worse than term-limits in CA, it seems to me, is the Prop 11 (?) property tax limit. In effect it accomplishes just what Bush [wishes] by precluding public progress by increasing the debt to eliminate all room for discretionary spending. Tax cuts for rich people have a dual purpose.

Kristof's article in today's NYT (Fri) is very depressing. It really shows how the master salesman from Texas can get away with magic. Max Weber had the key to it all: we are the Protestant country par excellence, even without depending on consciously Protestant voters. It all reminds me, by various contrasts, of our Emerson topic. He took a different turn, but his doctrine – misprised as it may have been – encouraged the distorted individualism that leads to the dysfunctional "federalism" of public utilities, public health, and "states rights" in general. "Devolution" suits our plutocrats as well as it suited the English barons fighting their kings.

However, in so far as I deserve any right to judgment based on reading a few of the essays many years ago, I agree with your admiration of his innovative literary talent, which was slightly soured for me only when I came across one or two of his wrongheaded ideas about this or that. In fact, I was quite enthusiastic about some of his insights and locutions.

I happen to be reading Max Weber now (for the first time), who has our sociopolitical seeds in his exceedingly convoluted nutshell. His famous "Protestant ethic" is far too complex to be bandied about as it is. He sheds a lot of light on the concept(s) of transcendentalism, the use, abuse, and ambivalent use of which intrigues me.

I'll always be glad to hear more from you about it. I suppose I ought to read Perry Miller too.

... I assume *The House of Dogs* is something you want to translate. Or did you write it yourself?

I have just finished a genuine work of art about the Shoah, by Kertesz, a Hungarian Nobel Laureate whom I'd never heard of.

Do you know it? It's not like any other that I know of, even Primo Levi's.

Do you happen to know any English-to-Arabic translator. An Iraqui woman who's head of the English Dept at Bahrain Univ is interested in my two plays about Gilgamesh, and just at this time the Iraquis are said by journalists to be desperate for cultural respect to overcome their humiliation. The serious difficulty of course is translation. I should think UNESCO would be interested in helping out.

August 15, 2003
To Richard Altobelli

Gore's Speech

I'm immensely pleased that you caught and appreciated Gore's speech. I read about it, read the full text word for word (the first time in my life doing such a thing), and then saw it all on C-Span. I printed out copies of it but didn't send one to you for fear of being mocked. I think it's a masterpiece of low-key moderate sober partisan rationalism.

Whether or not he or Clark gets "drafted", those two are my only present hope for winning the historically crucial 2004 election. (Read Kristof's 8-15-03 column in the NYT to see why I'm so scared for our country, and thus for the world.) Kerry would be a good president, my favorite of the nine, but I doubt that he can [beat] the master-salesman in voter sentiment. Dean is excellent, as far as he goes – an ideal Sec'y for the cabinet – but I think he'll falter in major-league hardball vs. Rove and the salesman. (All nine have good things to say, especially Kerry and Graham.)

See [Gloucester Democratic City Committee website] for something I wrote a couple of months ago.

... I thought you'd discontinued the Basilicum site, but now I see that it's still there. Cathy has signed me up for the domain name "gilgameshplays.net" and soon she'll have a web page to use it in.

She's acting as my agent for the two Gilgamesh plays (the second being from my Gmas work-in-progress).

Some serious interest has been expressed to my son-in-law by an Iraqui woman who's head of the English Dept at the Univ of Bahrain. The problem is to get a translator and take advantage of the Iraquis present desperation for national cultural respect at this time of their humiliation.

I'm sorry about Carleen. It must be very hard on you.

August 29, 2003
To Peter Anastas

Gore and Clark

I've been devouring and supporting the Clark movement – see the Web site via Google – for a long time with enthusiasm, and seen him on C-Span conducting a seminar, etc.

He's brilliant and charming, a real intellectual.

But I knew nothing about what you've just sent me! Is that from a British news service?

The NYT finally put Clark speculation on the front page yesterday. Tom Ashbrook had him on WBUR a few weeks ago. Clark has a book already in print and apparently a new one, or new pb edition, coming out in a couple of weeks. I have ordered them.

Did you read Gore's great speech a couple of weeks ago?

It's worth reading word for word. Kuttner made it his lead article in the latest AMERICAN PROSPECT. I'm enthusiastically for

EITHER or BOTH Gore and Clark! I'm hoping Gore will endorse Clark if he resists the Draft Gore campaign (also on the Web). Or that they somehow end up running as a ticket.

I'm very happy to know you're with me on Clark at least!

Let me know how to get to your source, which seems to be a scoop!

... As a birthday present to me (by pure coincidence), bring Judy to the Democratic Picnic at Stage Fort Park as my guests: SUNDAY, Sept 7, Noon-4 PM. Food will be provided.

Please let me know if you will come so that I can RSVP the logistical people.

PS: We need Kerry, Graham, Edwards, and Lieberman in the SENATE!

PPS: See the Clark quote, which I use with my email signature, below the message from you that I'm replying to.

"The United States is a 225-year rolling revolution...
We are the embodiment of the Enlightenment..."

– General Wesley Clark

August 29, 2003

To Peter Anastas

1000% Superior to George II's

Thanks for the *Telegraph* tip. I'll try it myself. (I've found the *Guardian* technically inconvenient, compared to the NYT.) They seem to be ahead of the US press.

I am not yet prepared to give up my faith in Tony Blair. I suspect that he's been deceived, but his competence, values, and purposes are 1000% superior to George II's.

Yes, Dean is getting more convincing, more relaxed, and I hope less invidious about his Crat rivals. He's been superb as a Sec'y in Clark's cabinet! But I don't think he's experienced or chastened enough for foreign affairs, or for DC politics or the Cans' culture-juggernaut. His NYC speech was great on C-Span (which, next to the NYT, is the most useful medium in our media – if only it weren't limited to cable users.)

... I'll look for *The Emperor's Tomb*.

... I'm amazed about Albert. Thanks for reminding me of the precious past.

September 11, 2003

Tree-Root Politics
How Unenrolled Voters Can Be More Effective

Grass-roots politics may serve the purpose for immediate special causes or narrow temporary measures. But they die with the inevitable decline of enthusiasm, like grass at the end of its season. You have to start all over again for each new protest or special issue, for each separate cause or electoral candidate. But representative government is a seamless web of values and individuals continuously related to each other by cause and effect. How many citizens have the time or stamina for the perpetual enthusiasm or outrage of repeated or simultaneous grass-root campaigns?

It is much more effective to support as nearly as possible your entire set of values – if only by voting in regular elections – choosing candidates who are likely to reinforce each other, thus multiplying the weight of your single vote at the higher (and highest) levels of power. Such is the purpose of political parties. A consistent party slate, by and large, increases your political influence on the outcome of most or all the issues you care about – steadily and all year round, while you go about the business of daily living.

Not all Republicans think alike, but in effect all their local and state votes converge at the presidency. By the same token not all progressives are alike in opinions, but when all their votes converge within the breadth of the Democratic Party they can replace any regime in Washington that ignores the common good and defies its democratic allies.

This process of convergence outgrows and outlasts the life-cycle of level grass. Instead it resembles the life of a tree, whose roots join to form a trunk that supports and nourishes all the intertwined branches of government and public service – the whole lofty diversity of economic or cultural foliage.

If people of goodwill converge from their various but similar roots of interest, their community of values can rise like a hardy oak for all seasons, infinitely more representative of the common good than the uniform Republican spruce tree that's always green with dollars and pointed at the top. The Democratic oak symbolizes the realistic recognition of a colorful just society in all its complexity, from acorn to winter twigs and summer leaves, generation after generation.

But a citizen's goodwill tends to defeat its own purpose in casting votes simply on the basis of single issues or attractive personality. Each candidate for office is offered by a party. No political representative, at any level of office, whether or not privately in tune with that party on all issues, can help supporting the party's characteristic program. It's the winning party that controls the agenda of Congress through the all-important system of partisan committees, as well as the executive power that largely determines the supreme judicial power, not to mention military and international policies.

For instance, though it is true that a few Republican politicians are "environmentalists", your vote for one of them will ultimately contradict your will if you are seriously concerned about the present and future condition of Mother Earth, because that same person will support the Republican organization of Congress, as well as a Republican president whose appointments and executive orders repeal, prevent, or hinder ecological improvement and protection of all kinds.

By the same token, as a Democratic voter, one or more of your own particular interests, even if not of special interest to a majority within the party, can often be carried to fruition on the strength of your fellowship as a member of the generally unified political family. This principle has been demonstrated over the years especially in civil-rights and environmental legislation.

So every vote for the party rises all the way up from the deepest far-flung rootlets to the uppermost and outermost buds of social progress. That's the reason to *vote* for Democrats in every election.

But that's not all. The reason to *register* as a Democrat is that you can participate in the planting and fertilization of the roots themselves. Even if you already vote Democratic without choosing to identify yourself as one of us, and even if you never go to a Democratic meeting or contribute a nickel to the Party of a demographic majority, the addition of your name to the Democratic voting rolls will magnify your effect by impressing other voters with the viability of progressive party politics. The size of our partisan registry can warn Republicans to back off with their reactionary attacks upon the many generations of constructive accomplishments by our Party in both peace and war – and to moderate their determination to pack the courts with their "conservative" judges.

But above all, a larger official Democratic registration on the voting lists will encourage present Democratic office holders to be more outspoken in defending and proclaiming the values of a Party devoted to the common good, and in emphasizing what distinguishes us from Republicans.

It's a moral imperative to vote. It's a political imperative to register as a partisan.

September 30, 2003

To Tribune@theclarksphere.com

A New American Patriotism

Suspicious Democrats should remember "The Road to Damascus", when God suddenly struck Saul, the vehement persecutor of Christians, with 180 degrees of enlightenment! He immediately dedicated his immense ability and energy to the new religion, which soon recognized him as *Saint Paul.*

Clark of course is no saint, but he should be welcomed for his secular conversion, and his definition of a New American Patriotism that can be trusted! He was already enlightened about everything else; now he (like Tony Blair) knows that the charming cowboy has really been just a super-salesman all along. That kind of Republican deception is hard for true gentlemen to realize – but, once the deceit is recognized, a valiant gentleman responds like a knight!

November 14, 2003

To George Hochfield

Achievement in Diplomacy

Re: Your earlier message, asking my impressions:

Yesterday I went to our pub. library and found the article you were speaking of. I'm very glad you told me about it because it was full of details that I'd been looking for. But I don't think it was "typical" of retired general at all. (Nothing about WSC is typical). I was in a sense somewhat reassured because it demonstrated that dimension of his social ability at a time when the military establishment is girding up to get its revenge for his maverick-success in balking it in the Balkans, where his achievement in diplomacy (and disciplined Army semi-insubordination) is probably unprecedented in history.

That war was far more complicated than the present one because it was internationally cooperative. He was an intellectual man of action beholden to half a dozen different democratic governments, always farsighted in concern for humanitarian values. (He has always paid a lot of attention to the personal and social welfare of our soldiers.)

But the reason I'm not as alarmed as you are about his (comparatively) modest gains in wealth is that he clearly remains much more interested in public service than in personal acquisition of money, and that it's coming primarily from professional services in innovative small business at the sub-contract level where the enterprises tend to be truly "free" (competitive). He doesn't work for the economic royalists. A lot of his money comes from writing and speaking about public affairs, past and present.

Anyway, most of his enemies represent the oligarchy.

Nevertheless, I can see why any liberal who hasn't read his books or followed him closely on C-Span should be leery. This Sunday he'll be on Meet the Press (which I've never seen before), and I'm anxious about how well he defends himself from our side of the spectrum. If he succeeds at that he can beat the Bush side of it with less difficulty.

November 27, 2003

To Mark Power

Losing Substantial Confidence in Blair

Happy Memories of American Thanksgiving!

I've just read that there are a quarter of a million Americans living (working?) in Britain. I hope they all vote – insofar as they are not duped by GWB.

I'm finally losing substantial confidence in Blair. I still think his social motives are decent. He'd make a good Democrat over here, diametrically opposed to Republicanism; but when he invites Bush to his own home precinct as a personal guest I'm really dismayed! Like some of our good Senators he'd trusted the word of our president, but now it appears he's essentially (not just as worthy diplomatic expedience) misjudged our salesman and his motives.

I know you've long since discounted Blair's motives from the point of view of Brit domestic politics; now I'm sadly catching up with you from a greater distance. The world really needs someone with his ability and ultimate international goals but without his stubborn gullibility, especially if Bush gets reelected.

Please correct my remaining misapprehensions!

c. next June I hope to be in the British archipelago, esp. the IOM, and Scandinavia. Will you be at home for a day's visit?

I'd like to meet your wife at last. I yearn for those isles of faltering transportation.

December 2, 2003

Letter to editor, *The Nation*

Moral Courage as a Keenly Responsible Leader

In *The Nation*'s attack on Wesley Clark one cannot recognize the one man of personal action who has done more than any other in this generation to implement the liberal values of Western civilization at its very center.

He may not please absolutely categorical pacifists, but as Supreme Commander of NATO in a Balkan war waged explicitly for human rights he encouraged the European Union and the divided United Nations at a time of excruciating uncertainty. He performed as an exceptionally skillful negotiator in obtaining and leading the willing military cooperation of many nations with differing political or cultural interests. In that part of his job he reported to NATO.

At the same time he was primarily but separately responsible to the civilian government of the US, through a chain of command that was abused by the Pentagon (under a Republican Secretary of Defense in Clinton's cabinet). The Joint Chiefs of Staff had little interest in foreign human rights, and were essentially opposed to a war authorized by the President in accordance with a moral foreign policy. In its necessarily complex directives to General Clark our prevailingly anti-intellectual Army did its best in Washington to mute the delicate international concerns of the President and the State Department which Clark as field commander fully appreciated.

Can one imagine a more difficult assignment? Yet the Kosovo war was a nearly bloodless success, thanks to Clark's intellectual capacity, incessant work, broad knowledge, strategic wisdom, and internal as well as external diplomatic ability. His analytical writings and speeches demonstrate a mind far broader than his military career.

Most admirable, however, is his moral courage as a keenly responsible leader often painfully alone in creative, respectful, and disciplined opposition to much of the military hierarchy of which he was such a distinguished part. He is no privileged aristocrat with the implicitly conservative support of a whole social class to embolden him – as, for instance, Douglas MacArthur considered himself to be. Wesley Clark's active mind is an exception to psychological archetypes.

[I'm surprised at *The Nation* for printing and glorifying the snide and smart-alecky opinions of a journalist ignorant about his subject, especially one who by his own admission sneaks into a presidential campaign like an FBI agent at some anti-war rally to pick up telltale quotes in the crowd.]

December 9, 2003
To a friend

Coming Election Is Our One Hope

I'm sorry you have had such a sad year. I didn't know about your daughter. Still less did I suspect that you and Ann have been having such a dismal time. But at least you're still painting, seeing that art is the only thing more important than politics. The market for art be damned!

For me the conflict between art and politics is excruciating, on behalf of the whole world, which Bush is disuniting. The Republican program of DEBT AND DECEPTION is a juggernaut to disaster, reflecting all rottenness of our American culture, which cannot distinguish between the polar opposites: advertising and education.

This coming election is our one hope. I fear that Gore's endorsement of Dean will carry the Democrats into one more electoral failure. He's a good man but he cannot beat Bush. Much as I favor Gore above all the candidates as a president, I think he's mistaken in this endorsement, pragmatically speaking.

Who is your favorite?

And does Ann agree?

December 12, 2003

To Mark Caggiano

A Few Pins and Stickers

I forgot to tell you that I missed seeing you at the recent Boston fundraiser, at which I got to shake the hero's hand. But there were plenty of people who looked as if they might be professional colleagues of yours.

Gore's endorsement might turn out to be of advantage of Clark by getting his other rivals to gang up on Dean, splitting their votes, don't you think? Especially if the Clintons are promoting Clark among contributors behind the scene.

Question: Is it true that we have to get 15 percent of the Primary vote in MA in order to [get] even a single delegate?

Question: Catherine and I hope soon to hold a small fundraiser here, but without waiting for an official "kit" how is it possible to order a few pins and stickers, even yard signs, for our friends?

Our chant about Bush should be

DEBT AND DECEPTION!

Maybe we could have an open contest for other such refrains.

December 28, 2003

To downloads@clark04.com

Debt and Deception

Let Wesley Clark Repeal Bush's Program of DEBT AND DECEPTION

[I.e., emphasize Republican violation of their own stated values, and their inconsistencies about "States Rights" and human rights in dictatorships.]

December 31, 2003

To Celia Eldridge

Concern for the International Environment

I think Wesley Clark is going to be Dean's surviving rival, until their positions are reversed. I believe the conventional opinion is right: that Dean will be too weak in the south, and elsewhere beyond our liberal pale, to beat Bush.

At this stage the domestic differences among the Crat candidates don't matter as much more than hypothetical hopes, because their criticisms of Bush and their values (for the Common Good) are essentially similar; AND because all those matters, vitally important as they are, have to go through the grinder of Congress, debate, and compromise.

Any Crat president is likely to have many of the same expert advisors. (Clark already knows a lot about social welfare from his experience as a base commander (="governor") in various places dealing with education, physical and mental health care, housing problems, and other family matters, in which he took a keen interest, conspicuously considerate of the pursuit of happiness by the lower ranks.)

But in foreign and Defense affairs a president has tremendous autonomy, and that's where an exceptional individual's intellect, ability, competence, character, temperament, leadership (largely by teaching), experience with international and humanitarian complexity, and personal wisdom, are all-important – because less beholden in advance to Congress or public opinion. I simply cannot imagine Dean fulfilling those requirements as well as Clark. And that's why Clark, as a leader of extraordinary ability, is probably the only Crat who can beat the promotional sentimentalism of Bush's misleading program DEBT AND DECEPTION.

But among Clark's domestic political virtues (which are by no means separate from the international ones), are his inside knowledge of business and finance (especially the entrepreneurial kind), of Pentagon planning and procurement, and of Budget Office/-Capitol Hill politics. (Remember how FDR put Joe Kennedy, a Wall Street shark, in charge of the SEC to clean it up?) I can hardly imagine Dean leading the Military-Industrial Complex in either peace or war.

Then too, I believe, Clark's really heartfelt concern for the international environment as the ultimate issue for the next hundred years, would be addressed in a way similar to the manner of Environmental Defense [Fund] – with a diplomacy of hardheaded cooperation, negotiating progressive and regulated incentives between unselfish people and characteristically selfish corporations or business associations. The Cans are always going to be the economic oligarchs of America, so we need a people's tribune who understands how to use their managerial ideology against them.

Clark is a very quick read in almost any subject, and he's a master at extrapolating his actual experience to other fields. I've read both his books and seen him for hours on C-Span in all sorts of situations, so I feel as if I've studied him personally!

Dean is surly or stupid to criticize Clinton for merely halting the Raygun Revolution, instead of reversing it. It took Clinton the David to stop that Goliath in his tracks. Now that the giant's sons are forcing us further back, Clark is the only one who as president has the ability to "Turn Around" (as he puts it) the battle from where Clinton left off – leadership UP hill rather than DOWN hill!

January 4, 2004
To friends

Clark's Strength as a Leader

Please forgive me if you don't want messages like this from me. Just reply with one line, saying "no more!" No offence will be taken.

On the other hand, feel free to forward any of my messages to anyone if you wish.

My daughter Catherine and I recently gave a Clark "Houseparty" to raise money for him. I think he's going to be Dean's surviving rival, until their positions are reversed. I believe the conventional opinion is right: that Dean will be too weak in the South.

The domestic wish-list differences among the Democratic candidates basically don't matter at this stage as much more than hypothetical hopes, because their criticisms of Bush and their values (for the Common Good) are essentially similar; AND because all those issues have to go through the grinder of Congress, debate, and compromise. Clark's strength as a leader provides a much greater possibility of implementing domestic reform.

In international affairs a president has tremendous autonomy, and that's where this man's intellect, ability, competence, character, temperament, experience with diplomatic and humanitarian complexity, and personal wisdom will firmly establish his overall leadership. He will then be less hindered by Congress or political opposition to internal national progress. I simply cannot imagine Dean matching Clark in those qualities. And that's why Clark is the only Democrat who can expose and turn around the Bush administration's DEBT AND DECEPTION.

Among Clark's domestic political advantages are his inside knowledge of business and finance (especially the entrepreneurial kind), of Pentagon planning and procurement, and of Budget Office/Capitol Hill politics. I can't imagine Dean leading the Military-Industrial Complex in either peace or war.

Then too, I believe, Clark's really heartfelt concern for environment as the ultimate international issue for a hundred years would be addressed with a sophisticated and forceful diplomacy of cooperation, with incentives between unselfish people and naturally selfish businesses. Clark is capable of holding the energy barons to much higher "clean skies" promises.

Clark is a very quick study in almost any subject, and he's a master at extrapolating his actual experience to other fields. I've read both his books and seen him for hours on C-Span in all sorts of situations, so I feel as if I know him personally.

Dean shouldn't have criticized Clinton for halting the Reagan Revolution without reversing it. It took Clinton the David to stop that Goliath in his tracks. Now that the giant's sons are forcing us further back, Clark is the only one who as president has the ability to "Turn Around" (as he puts it) the battle from where Clinton left off – leadership UP hill rather than DOWN hill!

January 24, 2004
To Ina Hahn

Toward True Philosophical Patriotism

Yes, dear Ina, as we move south and westward there will be less suspicion of a military man and more of the "93% liberal" (which I am, of course) Kerry. The American electorate is sentimentally patriotic and Clark is the one to steer it toward true philosophical patriotism before it realizes that he's an over-educated intellectual. It will take a little more time for voters to understand his amazingly broad competence, but at least they're already impressed by West Point, NATO command, or the medal Clinton awarded him.

I've read both his books (no mere campaign autobiogs) and watched him closely for many hours on C-Span, as well as twice extensively witnessing his performance within handshake distance, so I know him better than the pundits do. In person (rather than in formal speeches or "gotcha debates") he's irresistibly charming and creatively informative. His position statements are comprehensive and innovative on domestic as well as international matters.

The Republicans are really scared of running against him. You can spot this every time you see a conservative shill or a Republican newspaper (like ours) judiciously endorse one of the others they'd love to see up against Bush.

January 30, 2004
To Torsten Kehler

Our Only Hope

I'll have a Scotch and water.

I am touched by your cordial message.

If it weren't for art, as Nietzsche said, life would be unbearable. But in the USA, especially at this moment in world history, politics is more important than art. So it grieves me to find you so mistaken about American government. I think it's partly because you are born to the European parliamentary model of a political spectrum of Left and Right, with all its particular gradations within a mature culture – where, for instance, "conservative" retains much of its literal meaning.

(One thinks of Burke.) In this country the "right", with few exceptions, is literally reactionary – a very different adjective.

I don't think you understand our "right" in its psychological essence of selfishness, originally justified in spiritual terms by the Reformation, transferred from religious to secular ideas, and extended broadly into our current version of exceptional nationalism. God knows we needed the Reformation to check superstition and authoritarianism, but in doing so most of our country (as a Protestant nation to this day despite its misguided Roman Catholic voters) has lost the concept of the common good in its pursuit of happiness through an individualism owing more to usury than to humanitarian values.

The boats of both our parties float on the tide of a corrupted culture that reflects its anti-educational broadcast advertising and its stratified usury. They must be compared with this in mind. I cannot defend the Democrats against their necessary participation in popular culture and the sloppy language that prevails. I defend them politically as our only hope for the conservative preservation of the progress we have made in complex democracy and for further progress in humanitarian enlightenment (which you scorn in Carter and his ilk).

You seem to believe Republican talking and ignore their walking. (Bush and all his "neo-conservative" knights are all in their varying degree direct products of Republican metamorphed theology.) Can't you see how phony almost all their crusades for "freedom and democracy" are? Study their definitions! Study their motives? What's the distinction between "freedom" and selfishness (whether personal or extended, material or spiritual)?

About the only really moral issue the Cans have is abortion (and I'm respectfully against the sincere ones on that).

Bush's DECEPTION and DEBT mocks your conservative values. You should realize that the straw men you raise about silly Political Correctness and immature "liberals" are harmless in American political reality. I share your reaction against that, and your abhorrence of the stupid Left, American or French; but it's no real threat to the Common Good because it isn't basically selfish. Real "liberty" (not the Republican escutcheon) is intellectual, not commercial.

In all your tendentious surfing for turds at the bottom of the sea please enlarge the apertures of your net!

Dear Torsten, your amazing energy and genuine goodwill impel me to take all this time to hunt-and-peck my keyboard. You are a good cosmopolitan but you are overweening about American politics. Please try to understand Republican DEBT and DECEP-TION. ("Free Enterprise" comes from the mouth of a Trojan Horse made in America.) Then I'll defer to you in your estimations of European socialism.

My time shrinks more rapidly than yours. I hope you won't mind the efficiency with which I'm sending my thoughts by a copy of this to your loyal and highly respectful friend Gary.

I do hope you get a job close enough for more direct conversation. You know, I've hardly mentioned politics to Ralph, only to a friend of his who was with him when he called upon us this summer. But I'm in sympathy with your attitude toward what I surmise is his!

February 4, 2004

To Catherine Bayliss

A Candidate Who Can Win Over a Majority

At the moment Kerry is in the journalistic spotlight, just as Dean has recently been. With quiet right-wing assistance innocent lemmings are in a rush to follow him over a dark cliff. But it's not too late to turn on lights and prevent the national and international disaster of a Bush reelection. Kerry is a good man but he's highly vulnerable to Republican attacks.

With disingenuous advice from Republican pundits the press is making primary voters overlook the fact that in many states the Democrat voting runs exactly opposite to the majority in general elections. We need a candidate who can win over a majority of all the voters.

Wes Clark has had only four months to catch up on a year or two of campaigning, but he is a national floodlight. He can light up the whole stage if we continue to support him until reason and sanity are recovered in political consciousness one week at a time.

Don't let Democratic office-holders and advisors get carried away in a premature frenzy of assumptions or endorsements, just because journalists have been giving most of their attention to superficials.

Let's put on the headlights in Tennessee!

February 12, 2004
To Torsten Kehler and Gary Grieve-Carlson

The Real Issue about the War

May I butt in?

The real issue about the war is simple but too complex for the simpleminded voting public. Kerry, Clark, Biden and others who understand statecraft are still trying to find a way to break through the communication barrier in a sentimental anti-intellectual and demotic culture:

Ignore the political fringes. At the political center it's not really war vs anti-war (as Dean and Kucinich have it) but the right vs the wrong TIME and WAY to go about removing Hussein (a tyrant probably worse than Hitler in personal cruelty), with vs without EFFICIENCY of humanitarian force, with vs without INTERNA-TIONAL approval, with vs without honorable MOTIVE, with vs without moral SINCERITY, with vs without worldly and proleptic WISDOM.

"What's the rush?" as I wrote to our local paper before Bush got his way.

All my life I've been an imperialist, inviting equal Congressional and electoral votes to every unforced applicant according to our Constitution, starting with British Columbia and the Maritimes! Think how it would enrich our culture and sophisticate our politics! We might even get a Canadian president. And EVENTUALLY have two senators from Sumer! Maybe even Ireland would sign on. I would hope for a British Chief Justice.

February 13, 2004
To Torsten Kehler

It's the Salesman's Duplicity

I agree about trusting Blair. But Blair trusted a gentleman's agreement with Bush, as did Kerry and many other Democrats when he gave private assurances of cautious motives. It's the salesman's duplicity (justified by God's secret Calvinist "calling") that infuriates his critics. (Not to mention, domestically, his egregiously dishonest career beforehand.) You have no idea of what damage he's done to American society with the hypocrisy of his chrematistic religion.

The entire removal of Hussein could have been accomplished in little more time than this without his anti-social Debt and Deception. His immediate response to 9-11 deserves no special praise. Any other president would have done at least as much in patriotic "leadership."

February 13, 2004
To John Hlinko

Would Make a World-Respected Team

I am one of your very grateful early followers. No one exceeds me in admiration of Wes Clark.

Kerry was my second choice. I'm delighted that Clark has promptly endorsed him. They would make a world-respected team. Aside from "Southern strategy" and all the rest of conventional wisdom about electability, it's after winning the White House that Clark's worth as a national treasure would be resoundingly evident, especially in case of a national emergency. Kerry will need strong executive and international assistance, especially in managing the military-industrial behemoth. It's hard to imagine any other Democrat doing so well in assuming the present powers of Cheney or Rumsfeld or Powell.

Can you personally do anything to promote this reminder in such a way that Kerry will appreciate the additional support he would earn from professional and business groups, as well as ordinary citizens, by looking that far forward even right now?

Of course Kerry will first need Clark's help (especially as a running mate) to win the election, because as a Senator and "liberal" he is very vulnerable to misunderstood positions he's taken in his recorded votes over many years.

May your patriotic movement never fade away!

(Please feel free to quote me, directly or indirectly, in whole or in part, edited or unedited, anonymously or otherwise, if you find it of any help – especially for Kerry's ears!)

February 18, 2004

To ClarkDemsMa@yahoogroups.com

Must Keep Singing WKC's Praises

We may be approaching an unlikely but very alarming situation. If Kerry (whom many of us support as our second choice) somehow falters or fails, or if there's some kind of personal disaster before the Convention, we certainly don't want to find ourselves with a weak or unsuitable candidate who simply happens to be the last man standing, especially one who has been bolstered by malicious Republican votes in open primaries.

The only thing that matters is delegate counts. We have merely 71 as a limited base, but it's enough to attract augmentation from desperate groups in a political emergency. And we can pick up a few more apportioned from remaining primaries. (We should especially try to get some from the forthcoming MA primary.)

Above all, however, not only are the numerous ex-officio national delegates free to switch (or stick to Clark) at the Convention, but so (I believe) are those of all or most of the other delegates remaining from also-rans like Clark. The end-game might still be open to negotiation – if only to prevent the nomination from going to a disastrous candidate – that is, to one other than Kerry (if for some unforeseeable accidental reason he's out of the picture).

In any case, we want to make Clark well known (as he still isn't) to national voters and politicians alike – for the sake of getting him some important position in Washington. Don't forget that he attracts more unenrolled and Republican interest than any of the others we have, including Kerry himself. Those voters will become more and more important as the nation grows increasingly critical of Bush's DEBT AND DECEPTION ...

We must keep singing WKC's praises! Please forward the substance of this reminder to every friendly voter (or future voter) you know.

March 4, 2004
To Torsten Kehler

If We Are to Save Civilization and Mother Earth

The other day I was interested in your point about poor slobs (as distinguished from the less obvious "middle class" slobs). Like you, I hate to see them at the check-out counter or slouching at their TVs or overfeeding their obese kids. But you're observing a cultural rather than a political horror. We in the USA all float (with or without horror) on that democratic culture of ignorance, self-interest, and semantic sentimentality – a culture in which broadcast advertising directly opposes and outweighs education. (I mean education as properly directed to engender critical thinking, not just as vocational training.)

Millions of prosperous citizens largely encourage and live off the food and drug industries that are encouraged to produce toxic or wasteful consumerism at every level. Educators hardly protest, lest Business eliminate liberal education entirely. The cause-and-effect of democratic society (the best that's possible) is so circular, from generation to generation, that it becomes the devolution of selfishness if the people aren't wise enough to elect governors primarily interested in the common good.

Ungoverned rule of the market economy allows for all sorts of "efficiency" only in suboptimized entities (companies, classes, families, individuals). By the law of nature, this counter-entropy (as in physics) increases the social entropy in its surroundings: hence poor uneducated self-defeating slobs breeding more of their kind. If we are to save civilization and Mother Earth we must increase the scope of each optimization and thus displace as much entropy (disorder) to the greatest possible circumference of geo-humanity, flora and fauna ultimately included.

That requires a great leap in the art and motive of management – especially by learning to measure efficiency in new (especially non-monetary) ways. I know that is possible. Measurement must be applied at higher and higher levels of optimization. Politicians must be obliged to measure for the future beyond their terms of office, increasing the span of their suboptimization in time as well as space.

At present the military (especially the Navy with ships as entities) demonstrates what's possible. It doesn't measure its efficiency in dollars only. Of course even the Navy as a whole is still a suboptimization because it spins off entropy into the environment (when it doesn't go so far as to destroy artifacts and kill humans, the ultimate creation of entropy).

But we can only hope for one entity, one industry, one alliance, one world-organization at a time. We degenerate in the other direction if we refuse to educate the poor as a social duty that threatens the suboptimization of the marketplace.

[The above impromptu screed only hints at a long essay that I won't live to write.]

March 5, 2004

To Torsten Kehler

Temperamentally a Meliorist

The new element in history is untaxed and unregulated broadcast commercial advertising in the USA.

I was not talking about English-major education. I meant demotic education (99% of the mass).

Every sine wave can be Fourier-analyzed as the sum of small waves.

Our overall curve can be going down at the same moment that some of the component waves are ascending. We have greatly improved human rights, medicine, nutrition, international cooperation (but not in the last three years), animal welfare, open attitudes about sex, communication, et al. And some nations have improved their territorial suboptimization, etc. But on a global basis, especially because of Bush's suboptimization, the health of Mother Earth (like that of international relations) is deteriorating, mainly because the US bulks so large, and because the limited surface of the earth cannot match even linear growth of the world population's self-optimizing individuals. If he wins again the slope of the enveloping curve will surely tip to the negative.

I'm temperamentally a meliorist (not an optimist) only because I'm limited by my own sphere of suboptimization.

Maybe your psyche is parallel in form if not in content!

August 1, 2004

To Peter Anastas

Convention Served Its Purpose

Virginia is the only name I could think of, but I rejected it as a false association of that state, to which they will be returning!

Thanks. I don't know what I'd do without you as my dear old adviser on many topics!

My research on the IOM was very rewarding, as well as a couple of days in Ireland and elsewhere ad lib.

... The convention served its purpose very well, despite the pundits. Obama, Clark, and half a dozen others were exciting too. I hope the DNC keeps a TOTAL tape of the whole thing, for future piecemeal use. The general public was deprived of most of it. No one who didn't keep on C-span missed many of its most interesting parts. (The one advantage I had as an invalid!)

God bless Krugman in the NYT! And Obama is more of a true intellectual than any of the other wiseacres. This world-political anxiety is excruciating. What else but a tipping or non-tipping point in modern history?

August 19. 2004

Letter to editor, *Gloucester Daily Times*

Practical Politics Is Party Politics

Like Ralph Nader, it's Jim Munn himself who needs the "reality check" he calls for in his latest column. He's like a cat who starves himself by refusing to eat the ordinary cat food provided by his benefactors. In our naturally imperfect democracy his scorn of practical politics only plays into the hands of those who obstruct an evolutionary path toward his own recognition of "the common needs of all humanity". Since we are not ruled by philosopher kings, progress must be practical at the citizen's level of existing conditions.

He's right that we should never forget the faults in our nation's history, but his review of them omits the fact that most of what he deplores was over the objections of many Americans at the time. They were out-voted or misled by those in power. As the organized or unorganized protesters they were simply not strong enough in practical politics.

Practical politics is party politics. Munn alludes to it only as "all the bickering and childish mudslinging every four years". But parties are coalitions of voters sharing certain general or particular values or ideas. In every democracy parties are as necessary for consistent progress as they are for effective opposition to progress, as in our case of Democrats versus Republicans. The "bickering" is usually about the devil's details that represent unstated motives or constitute the substance of very serious public policy.

Even though every legislation results from some degree of collaboration and compromise (especially in the foreign affairs of our nation as a whole), nothing in the reality of American political and economic life can be clearer in actual results than the broad distinction between Democrats and Republicans. Voters who split their tickets, or who regard themselves as "independent" because they choose randomly on the sole basis of attractive personality, in the end will usually thwart their own political logic, directly or indirectly, by supporting objectives that contradict each other.

That's because no official of any party can help contributing to the whole food chain of its organization, from bottom to top. The financial and ideological commitment of every member is what determines a vast range of detailed partisan issues, which in their entirety are beyond the grasp or even the personal interests of many legislative colleagues, who simply must trust in the expert knowledge and opinion of specialized partisan colleagues (as, for example, in tax law or military technology). Modern industrial democracy is much too complex to be mastered in all its aspects by any individual at any level of authority, even in the laudable hopes of idealistic observers like Jim Munn.

Jim should ask Bruce Tarr to explain why he is a Republican, necessarily committed to the Bush food chain.

Likewise he should ask Paul McGeary, who is running against Tarr for our State Senate, why he is in the Democratic food chain. With crystal clarity McGeary will explain his commitment, as a mainstream Democrat, to contesting a popular incumbent Republican. Paul is a bright new political light in our district, extremely well informed and extraordinarily articulate. He should be given a chance to prove himself a very productive member of the food chain that extends by way of Beacon Hill from Tony Verga to John Tierney, to Ted Kennedy, and finally to John Kerry as President.

It would be a civic education for Jim and all the rest of us to hear a debate between these two honorable partisans.

September 3, 2004
To Torsten Kehler

Their Grand Plan for an "Ownership Society"

Thanks for the emollient reply. I'm glad to know more about what you're doing sans Web.

I'd have to say Hamlet, Macbeth, Othello, Lear. At least the middle two had the makings of a hero. They were professionally competent. As far as I can remember (not having re-read any of them for many years), Lear had little or nothing to admire. (I'd like to know what Gary thinks.) The great advantage you teachers have is that you really know the material you talk about! My narrow tragic archetype (if confined to stage) is Oedipus and a few other Greek plays, besides Yeats. Possibly a Spaniard or two. Can't right now remember others. Your other advantage is that you obviously read twice as fast!

Ditto, me with you, about Nietzsche in general. But *Birth of Tragedy* is really important, worth (in my limited readings of him) all the rest of his creativity. Even though nowadays it seems weird, it should be revisited – along with Jane Harrison and Yeats's essays, as well as Lord Raglan, the amateur anthropologist – by drama theorists like Else.

... Your remarks on the BC Provincial Tories: it's just a tiny sample of what the Cans have been doing down here, much of it by unnoticed "executive orders" or outright secrecy, all part of their grand plan for an "ownership society", part and parcel of their international policies. Tories in England are pussy-cat gentlemen compared to almost all our "conservatives".

September 11, 2004
To Torsten Kehler

Apotheosis of Selfishness

I should have put "Ownership Society" in double or triple quotation marks. You have to understand what Bush (and Gingrich, et al.) mean by it. The same goes for many of their other slogan-terms, like patriotism, freedom, etc. His "ownership" is an apotheosis of selfishness. The key to American politics lies in motivational psychology. I guess it's hard for you more civilized people to see without having been saturated with it on the inside. It can be analyzed by social theory from the outside but not understood existentially by people of goodwill.

The common good is best served by regulated capitalism, which doesn't require selfishness or self-aggrandizement at all levels to maintain justice for the common good. I can't imagine Keats or Mother Teresa if they'd been preoccupied with the stock market, real estate, and tax exemptions to stay alive.

Please parse the rhetoric of Republican doctrine.

... But speaking of Shakespeare, have you seen Gopnik's review of Greenblatt's book in the latest *New Yorker*? What is your expert opinion of it? For me it's the best piece on Shakes that I've ever read. I wish I had time to reread all the plays mentioned.

September 28, 2004
Letter to editor, *Gloucester Daily Times*

Crocodile Tears about Integrity in Journalism

Gail Mountain's letter of Sept. 27 brings up the serious political problem of professional integrity in print and broadcast journalism.

All too often political argument is treated as if the two sides in a campaign are a couple of football teams playing by the same rules. In the name of "impartiality", irresponsibly malicious statements are given the same weight as claims of fact or reason. Apparently many journalists have never learned (or are forbidden to practice) critical thinking, the fundamental purpose of education.

Propaganda, the clever manipulation of words, deliberately confuses truth with lies, or distorts the meaning of accidental uncertainties. Take as a typical example the manner in which Republicans have exploited the technical error of CBS's Dan Rather. They use it to neutralize rational criticism of their Swift Boat conspiracy. Most journalists have apparently fallen for a false analogy between the two cases.

CBS may have been duped into accepting a document that embarrasses George Bush, but the substantial truth of its content has been readily affirmed by the very secretary whose verification of the forgery has been at least tacitly accepted as the last by almost everyone involved in the matter. No one doubts George Bush's abuse of special privilege and the rules of military service. One of the ironies is that investigative reporting by three or four of the country's leading newspapers had previously substantiated the allegations against Bush's behavior.

Likewise, investigative reporting had already discredited the Kerry-hating Swift Boat conspirators as outright liars about the very essentials of their propaganda. It was so obvious that official Republicans were embarrassed. Many unofficial Republicans seemed ashamed of that effort to discredit a true war hero whose early career so clearly contrasted with Bush's.

Republicans shed crocodile tears about integrity in journalism, and dupe most reporters into wiping the morality slate clean, practically exonerating the scurrilous Swift Boat gang as no worse than Dan Rather's. They so intimidated the head man of CBS, a professed Democrat, that he's pledged his vote to Bush.

Such is the financial power of the GOP.

Carl Rove knows perfectly well that the two cases are not parallel. It's the same indirect subversion of justice that often fools or intimidates much of our public information media. Republicans play by their own rules, abetted by purblind field officials.

November 5, 2004

To Catherine Bayliss

Define the Common Good

All we have to do now is find a way to define the Common Good for the common mind as incorporating ALL elements of the nation as an organic whole of our parts, including those not necessary for mere survival, such as fingers, legs, ears, and eyes – not just heart, lungs, liver, and brain.

I first heard the term as Thomas Aquinas's. He said it in context of feudalist hierarchy, but it can be applied even better to the more truly organic modern democratic body politic (as I suppose many liberal Catholic thinkers do nowadays). Once it becomes a familiar code-phrase (as defined by us) it can serve as a framework to interrelate all the policies, programs, proposals, and values we endorse as a democratic synthesis to everybody's long-term advantage in a patriotic society, rather than a mere collection of private self-interests.

If only Soros or even Michael Moore (who writes better than he speaks), or somebody else, would establish a think-tank for advising the DNC along this line of research in the language of our latent political philosophy!

December 19, 2004

To Manfred Hegemann

Kerry Has Guts

Nice to hear from you, just as I was about to send my Christmas Greetings to you and Brigitte the same way! I am no longer capable of dealing with the holidays as I know I should.

I'm hypersensitive about my remaining time because I've still got too much to finish, almost too late. Every other worthy activity is in conflict, especially when I have to go to a doctor or dentist, who think their time is more important than mine.

(Nothing life-threatening so far, but a few minor nuisances. I do bless Medicare!)

Every day I agree with your parallels between Hitler's time and ours. This is a real test of democracy's resilience, which has been so seriously weakened by an educational system steadily corrupted by television and the whole anti-rational culture that supports it, and by sentimentalized (Biblicized) ideas of misplaced religion. There were so many different tactical choices during the campaign that any one Kerry made was bound to be a "mistake" if only because they all tended to conflict with each other. I think he put up a better fight than any of the others (besides Wesley Clark, perhaps) would have. He really does have guts. Anyway, it was a mistake, in my opinion, for the Democrats in general to seem to promote, rather than only tolerate, "gay marriage", instead of simply civil union.

Often they (not Kerry) seemed to ordinary people to *want* abortions. Language has been our undoing, versus the abuse of language, as it was for Hitler's liberal opponents.

I'm just beginning to read *Berlin in Lights, the Diaries of Count Harry Kessler (1918-1937)*. (I got it cheap from Barnes & Noble over the Internet.) It's a priceless account of those years by a liberal aristocratic diplomat of astounding intelligence – an excellent writer. Your father must have known him. It's as much about German culture as politics. I wish I had time to read it more than a few minutes a day. I wonder if the people working on your father's biography mention him?

... I'm sorry about your beautiful sister. When I was fifteen she seemed to me an auburn-haired goddess. Is her husband still running the apple orchard?

Weinachten! I wish we could be drinking beer together! Did I tell you about my aborted effort to reach the Hamburg Ratshaus?

December 21, 2004
To Peter Anastas

Economic Social Justice

The printout you got must somewhere in the heading show a site to go to.

It came to me by email from Torsten Kehler (Ralph's friend) who scours the Web for neo-con sources like Dalrymple, and whose whole political stand (unlike Ralph's) seems to me to be based on his hatred for academic "political correctness".

This is a good example of the reactionary (either/or) mind that is unable to cope with the simultaneity of two contrary ideas or values of equal weight, especially when each of them is taken to necessarily epitomize a whole spectrum of apparently related ideas.

That's why I am a main-line Democrat and an equivocating Episcopalian, even as I agree with what you say. Politically speaking, some things are more important than others, and, for example, the "political correctness" of homosexual "marriage" (for me an anthropological term), which I'm against, as distinguished from the justice of civil union, is not nearly as important as economic social justice to fight for, even though a vote for one may be a vote for the other. So also, the language miscalled "*political* correctness". Dalrymple, who seems to have started out with exceptional goodwill, I think, knowing nothing else about him, is carried away by the slate of reactionary doctrine. We need an Elizabethan settlement, if only for the sake of successful democracy!

December 23, 2004
To George Hochfield

Don't Blame Kerry

How are you and Leonard making out with the various translations?

I was glad to hear (last June) that you at least are in basic good health. I have the usual harbinger checkups, but so far none of them are life-threatening. I do notice, however, that my credit card bills for medication (prescribed or not) are rising on a line like the national debt's.

My month overseas was more than half in the British Isles (which have become rather familiar as a whole), mostly on the Isle of Man for a meeting with the tiny George Borrow Society of English amateurs. I may go back again for a meeting in Wales next September if the dollar-exchange doesn't much exceed its present doubling of my expenses. (In such cases I just shorten my trips.) The Society, for me, is mainly just a social base at putative group-rates for lodging; but I do admire Borrow as England's nearest analogue (by a far cry) to Melville. Afterwards I got my first look at the southeast coast of England.

... Don't blame Kerry. He came on strong at the end. For every loss (as well as every win) there are many co-determinants and therefore as many decisions to take when it comes to choosing tactics.

Afterwards we never know what would have happened with a different selection of choices (any one of which may necessarily exclude the alternatives). I don't think any Democrat (except maybe Clark) could have done any better. We lost, I think, because of the Republican-falsified Democratic aura of "political correctness", which I extend to cover the liberal fringe of basically non-political fanatics, who have been much more useful at attacking Republicans than in representing the basic Common Good, or in countering the narrow phoney "values" issue.

As usual (except for a few like Lakoff) we lose in part because of insensitivity to the importance of language in overcoming propaganda, especially when voters don't know their own real interests and don't care about the common good. I'd like to see Kerry get a chance to continue where he left off (on the rise). We can't afford to start all over again with every election. The Cans just continue with their cast of personae, and it's paid off for them. ... So saith the soothsayer!

But at least the pressure is off, as a loser, to get more private work done. I've fallen way behind at the age of 78!

Please give my greetings to Mayflower, and to the Nathans.

PS: For the first time in several dogs' age I'm excited about college football: Harvard almost in the big leagues and Cal NO.4 therein! The Cal quarterback is my new hero ...

January 31, 2005
To George Hochfield

Individual vs. Society

I'm really surprised about Schlesinger mentioning such a religious matter. I read the book many years ago but the paperback copy I now have is (to my surprise) abridged and has no index; so I can't pursue the matter. But from what you say it sounds as if his conversion had nothing to do with the really *really* essential difference between Catholics and Protestants from a sociological point of view (which seems to be totally lost upon the contemporary churches and as well their secular counterparts): individual vs. society = freedom vs. organization = selfishness (spiritual or banausic) vs. common good, etc. The confusion on both sides is the main thing that muddles our electorate.

I was hoping you would find that Brownson quit for the sake of the common good! We are indebted to Protestants (aka Republicans) for the now corrupted value known as freedom; and to the

Catholics (aka Democrats) for their long-since confused idea of the just society. (Of course these intellectual metastases go far back before colonial America.) I don't expect to convince you of this, but it explains my avid interest in your marvelous analysis of the rugged individualists at their best.) My arguments involve very complex linguistic cross-connections between the spiritual and the mundane. In my view most of the theologies miss their own boats.

I'm sure I was substantially right about the Melville quote, because I didn't say it was uttered during the Transcendental period. Probably it came much later. *Clarel*, if I remember dimly, did reveal some interest in the Catholic point of view, but it probably was not for the reason above. However, it is evident to me from most of his work that his sympathies and his intellect were at least half Catholic (or Judaic) in tendency. We must allow for the overwhelmingly Protestant aura that conditioned (far more than now) the "framing" of education, discourse, nurture, and philosophy. It seems to me that HM dived deeper than any of the others even though he had to use the usual spiritual terminology.

NB: I am now little-by-little rereading him, and in my tardy maturity I may have to take back some of my wishful thinking.

White Jacket will be for me a better key than *Moby Dick*. I'm not thinking of belief, faith, divinity, or personal salvation when I speak of religion anthropologically (or philosophically), but I grant you that HM, as you say, was. Yet it seems to me that his symbol-system, based on reality (as you put it), was uniquely religious.

And your email writing, also, is uniquely interesting.

February 8, 2005
To local Democrats

Our Political Philosophy

1.

It is good to see that many Democrats are now deliberating proposals or improvements for our strategy, tactics, themes, programs, message language, voter enrollment, value definitions, demographic research, and other aspects of Party-building.

We have relied too much on the assumption that present voters are aware of the Democratic legacy embodied in almost every element of national and international progress since 1932. Most of those who now vote Republican do not realize that their present good fortune and apparent economic independence stem directly from Democratic policies that Republicans are now dismantling or reversing under false pretenses.

We are facing an onslaught of reactionary ideology that has been quietly developed in private Republican institutions but is now empowered by voters who have been deceived by dishonest language or secrecy of intentions.

Our problem is basically educational, not in the history of our accomplishments but in *making known what we ultimately strive for in everything we do as a party.* It is not enough to fight a series of separate battles.

Republicans now have to their advantage an unwritten political philosophy based almost entirely upon economic individualism. We, on the other hand, have an unwritten philosophy, based upon values and needs of our whole open society, that is hardly recognized even by those who consistently support us.

The domestic New Deal, victory in World War 2, and international leadership were possible in a series of emergencies faced pragmatically (and often experimentally) with the common good in mind. FDR's political genius, and his posthumous influence, were so persuasive under those conditions that nobody had to ask our Party "*What do you stand for?*"

But now, as the party representing an open society, it's urgent for us to think in terms of an open political philosophy in order to answer that pertinent question in terms that can be easily understood.

Again, listing the important issues on which we take a position, though necessary in battle, is not sufficient to win the strategic war of ideas and ideals. Most national elections depend more upon short simple answers to the general question than upon tactical debate, which is always vulnerable to changing conditions or complex explanation, especially when repeated out of context. Over and over again, moreover, we see devastating distortions of simple positive or negative replies to simpleminded challenges.

Such pitfalls and trickery, or trivial mistakes, can be diverted, defended, or turned to advantage only by referring to a comprehensive philosophy that we stand for, simply expressed. But the summary of a philosophy does not lie in a rhetorical manifesto of hopes and dreams.

Our reply to the simple question – what our questioners want – is a brief description of how as well as what we think and feel about the American body-politic. It must be expressed in such a way as to have our *general meanings and motives intuitively grasped by the questioners,* so that when they later hear our various messages they will immediately recognize them as reinforcing each other in new bottles of old language.

Thus the immediate task for us is to develop and succinctly articulate (at least for ourselves) a general political philosophy to explain altogether our *general* motive, our *general* objective, and our *general* way to exercise the existing democratic means to apply our *general* patriotic beliefs. And then we must find ways to express that philosophy with metaphors, images, and analogies, as well as facts and reasons, that clearly distinguish us as a robust and genuinely compassionate party.

2.

In order to do so, however, we should force literal attention to our general but non-partisan purpose (in the words of the Preamble to the Constitution) "*to form a more perfect Union, establish Justice, insure domestic Tranquility, provide for the common defence, promote the general Welfare, and secure the Blessings of Liberty to ourselves and our Posterity* ..." (These words should put Republicans to the test every time they proclaim the virtue of selfishness!)

Then, having adopting this preamble, I suggest that we agree in a philosophy (whether or not it is formalized and published) that *distinguishes* our Party from the largely conflicting motives and values of the Republican coalition.

It should be pragmatic as well as idealistic, cogent and clear, open to unlimited discussion, and intellectually serious enough to be discussed and refined at academic levels as well as at our Democratic tree-roots. It must be positive enough to be useful in reversing the radically reactionary movements which are now about to sweep away the ideas and principles our progress has been built upon for over seventy years. The country is in immediate peril of losing its resistance to the kind of unreasoning propaganda that suffocates the Constitution we were born with.

Our Democratic political philosophy need not necessarily be preached, as such, outside the choir, or even mentioned in outreach to voters. Unless or until it takes the form of an official document it may well be inappropriate to invoke its existence in regional campaigning for Democratic candidates or causes. Its purpose, rather, would be to serve our tree-root activity as the trunk of its oak tree – a stem of intellectual strength that all members of the Party can tacitly subscribe to and keep in the back of their minds.

Therefore it would not demand inclusion of ideas or opinions that are open to debate or option among Democrats. For example, it probably would not take categorical stands on certain so-called social issues or religious concepts. Like a constitution, and unlike the legislation or legal decisions enacted under a constitution, it would stipulate only general abstract concepts, except when the Constitution makes specific determinations. Our Party is perhaps the largest as well as the oldest in the world, comprising a much greater variety of interests than our opposition does. Its philosophy must leave as much room as possible for divergent personal opinions.

It must be emphasized that the formation of an unofficial Democratic philosophy does not by any means deny or conflict with the crucial work that is now being done to "frame the argument" or to devise improvements in our political communications, strategies, and tactics – all of which are more important than ever. Nor does it imply objections to the methods or procedures which have recently strengthened our Party (despite a few problematic losses). With a liberal philosophy in our background for guidance or justification we are as free as ever to take initiatives, get tough, compromise when prudent, or fight without concession any measure or appointment that violates our fundamental principles of policy or justice.

3.

"What do we stand for?"

[Some topics and suggestions to be considered as elements of our political philosophy.]

We stand for the common good, for the commonwealth, for the nation as a whole – as an organic system within a global system:

... for stalwart "partisanship" when it's a question of right vs. wrong for a just society. (If we repeatedly split the difference we will steadily lose.)

... for honest use of language.

... for efficiently sized government to meet our needs, neither too large for individual freedom and economic initiative nor too small for national or international security, enforcement of justice, mutual protection of the global environment, or mandatory regulation of free markets.

... for constructively sympathetic public assistance to those in need, as poor or incapacitated individuals, as disadvantaged social classes, or as undeveloped nations.

... for continuous construction and maintenance of public transportation systems, rationally apportioned among those of land, sea, and air, and meeting or exceeding the world's highest standards for safety and efficiency.

... for a national energy policy (public and private) emphasizing conservation, efficiency, and reduced consumption.

... for public support of pure as well as applied science.

... for increased respect and encouragement of liberal education, culture, art, and the worthy professions that do not share commercial motives or rewards.

... for especially encouraging both inside and outside school walls the study of history and government.

... for universal health care and its nationally equalized infrastructure, together with restraints upon mercenary exploitation of medical necessities, scientifically and legally regulated under public health policy.

... for universal social unemployment, disability, and retirement insurance, coordinated with health-care insurance.

... for fully staffed and vigorous non-partisan public enforcement of tax law, fiduciary duty, security exchange rules, corporate law, public communication doctrines, free speech, civil rights, and mandates for protection of environment or natural resources.

... for equitable improvement of international free-trade regulations.

... for fullest possible participation in the United Nations and other international organizations for peace or global progress, as well as in military and diplomatic alliances with as many allies as possible, emphasizing international cooperation of banking and police.

... for strengthening and balancing all the components of Homeland Security, especially increasing attention to maritime shipping and to local "first responders" for natural or hostile emergencies.

... for encouraging the organization of trade and professional unions.

... for moral consistency between domestic and foreign policy.

... improvement of government accounting systems, financial controls, and auditing standards.

... uniform federal standards for voting.

... etc.

These initial suggestions are not offered in their order of importance or in finished form, and some important ones may have been overlooked. They may be eliminated, modified, expanded, or augmented after collective deliberation. But to serve their purpose they must remain abstract practical ideas, meant to avoid as far as possible particular concrete proposals in legislative or executive form. They are intended as a framework for practical politics within which the Democratic Party and its candidates can feel politically comfortable and flexible now or in the future.

We must leave ourselves at liberty to continue what we are already doing, and make the philosophy consistent with whatever of general importance may become necessary to express the soul of our Party.

4.

Naturally we can't reply to the question of what we stand for by reciting some such litany. We need at least *one central image that can be intuitively grasped by an ordinary semi-informed citizen,* whose main impressions are informed or misinformed in mass communications, or by the propaganda of carefully selected issues that are deliberately isolated (a la Carl Rove), omitting others that are of far more intrinsic importance.

So let us be the country's trusted Primary Care Physician who sees and treats us as whole human beings within in a whole human society. *Our doctor is a general practitioner for the nation's health, which depends upon the balanced interaction of all our organs, our nutrition, our social behavior.*

This metaphor applies almost exactly to our role in politics. Political philosophy and medical science are alike in this respect.

Republicans, on the contrary, at their best are specialists or pharmacologists who may or may not cure one organ at the expense of another simply because they are not thinking primarily of the whole body-politic. At their worst they maximize (in the short run) the performance of one organ or one sub-system, to the detriment of others, for their own special benefit.

Democrats want the common good, when all organs are working together in proper balance. Our Primary Care Physician knows what's more important than what isn't. Brains, hearts, lungs, and guts are more important than fingernails (which might be likened to tax cuts for the rich). When the body-politic is in proper health it's no longer business *versus* labor, or rich *versus* the poor, or security *versus* liberty, or conservation *versus* industry, or globalization *versus* full employment.

I believe that this kind of human imagery can be developed with various media, in many different aspects, and refined for public use as familiar icons of what we stand for. They would all fit well with the Preamble to our Constitution.

April 1, 2005

To Manfred Hegemann

Bush Is Pure Salesman

Good to hear from you! I was about to ask the same of you.

Yes, I read the *Times* (on the Web) every day and I'm addicted to Dowd (now that she doesn't have Clinton to jeer at).

The news is so bad about our country (from a world-historical point of view) that I can't help thinking it's going to start a revolution, but maybe too late – maybe, in the decline of culture, we've passed the tipping point. Bush is pure salesman, the epitome of intellectual corruption. And Robb (a nominal Democrat, son-in-law of HST?) lets him get away with it. But a few good voices are arising. The trouble is that they don't own the airwaves.

My best to Brigitte. Is Harto mellowing into old age, like you? I visualize all three of you in bird's-eye Shangri-La.

May 1, 2005

Kick from an Old Donkey

Republican pundits taunt us with not being able to say what we stand for besides criticism of them and opposition to their "reforms". They are half right. But even now, before the next election, we are winning on certain issues. We are regaining some old ground. We are better than we used to be at listing what we want for the common good – things we're for and things we're against.

Of course we must continue to do so in debate and in discussion with voters. We are starting to make the distinction between genuine political issues and the so-called "moral values" of religious fundamentalism, and to defend a reasonable understanding of the Constitution. Our electoral tactics are improving. Our tactics are improving.

However, we haven't yet found a concise and memorable Preamble, or intellectual umbrella, for our Party with which to answer the simple question of what we stand for. We need to show that our ideas are related to each other according to a political philosophy which can be named, recognized, and developed in think tanks and the public media.

It is hazardous to rely entirely upon a long or short list of what we approve, hope for, or resist. A list does not explain what the items have in common as our basic motivation or ultimate values. But, more important, in certain political situations (such as canvassing in the field) any list may omit or include individual items that are by themselves either objectionable or inexcusably missing to an individual voter. That voter, unless better informed than the average citizen, may very well happen to be preoccupied with that one cherished subject, even if it is actually of much less importance than all the others in the life of that same voter.

This political hazard is especially true in the case of so-called "moral values", and is well understood by Carl Rove's students. I believe that the Republicans won the last election precisely because they were careful not to expose their own main ideology. In clever mass mailings and rallies they segregated and selected specific target-groups, picking and choosing from their dictionary of inconsistent talking points.

The point is not that we should practice this kind of dishonesty, but that we should face up to the problem by making it clear to voters that our political philosophy is meant for an open society. Many good Democrats don't agree with every item on our typical lists because they understand that our objective is the common good. They know that we strive for the idea of a commonwealth as a community representing far more than half the population – and that there is plenty of room for collegial dissent about particular means to a common good that neglects no one's honorable interests. We are truly a democratic fellowship of motives.

June 11, 2005
To Gene Bailey

Crucial Need for a Political Philosophy

There's no one I'd rather hear from! It augments my will power, which (for a hermit) always needs help in the race against time.

Our summer has only just begun, suddenly warm even in the sea breeze. I pity you there in the middle west even as I envy the lovely spaciousness of your well-kept town that seems to know not littering.

I'm going to England–Isle of Man–Wales for the second half of September on the pretext of a three-day meeting of the George Borrow Society. I'm still hoping to approximate the book schedule I proposed to you – i e , to hand you a MS. some time in 2006. But the ending of such a lengthy fiction-scheme (the first and last of a crazy genre) is the most difficult part of all, especially considering the problem of consistency when one's memory is failing!

Please tell the AT that I'm still a hopeful fan of her compatriot Wes Clark, a dark horse that the country and the world desperately need on our 2008 ticket, with or without Hillary.

This country seems on the way to another 1929 (X 10). I think our Party is doing well right now from the bottom up, benefiting from the slow swing of public opinion, but at the top none of the Congressional leaders seem aware of the crucial need for a political philosophy – for an answer in Preamble to the question of what we stand for, not just lists of particular issues. We are for the common good, and that's what we should be defining.

Anyway, pondering that is the one thing that excuses the tardiness of my super-individualistic task!

Please come and talk about both these matters if you ever venture this far eastward before 2006. Above all, stay healthy!

June 2005

Second Kick from an Old Donkey

A majority of Americans are beginning to see through Bush and the narrow-minded arrogance of his headstrong administration. There is a good chance that their dishonesty will at last be recognized by a majority. But that doesn't necessarily mean that they'll vote for us in 2006 and 2008.

Howard Dean, the only one chosen to represent us all until we elect a president, is very actively extending and assisting a truly national Democratic organization. He emphasizes community. But he is not in a position to speak for our Senators, Representatives, or future candidates for office, though he and they substantially agree on issues, on objections to Republican folly, and on civic values.

But so far most of their lists of Party goals, in the form of "agendas" – intended for the common good – have been more appropriate for legislative debates than for a political philosophy that explains everything we stand for or oppose. Without such an explanation our ultimate motives won't be understood by people who vote against us because of a single issue. We lose elections when voters have no idea about what essentially distinguishes us from Republicans.

We must take the offensive by criticizing what we can see that Republicans actually stand for, not in rhetoric, but in what they do and hope to do. That will help us approach the task of articulating, in contrast, an open and honest political philosophy of our own. We must publicly question Republican motives and relentlessly criticize their propaganda.

The danger of "centrism" is that almost every step in that direction makes it harder for us to deny the moral legitimacy of Republican individualism especially when it speaks in the name of religions that urge quite the opposite of self-aggrandizement.

Maggie Thatcher (Reagan's soul-mate) said "There's no such thing as society, only the individual and the family." "God wants us to be rich" said a chaplain at a Republican Convention. Republicans even want privatized Social Security to accumulate heritable wealth for investors (instead of simply insuring retirement). What they mean is "We're all in this alone!" For them selfishness is a virtue, ownership more important than any other private right.

We must urge our leaders and think tanks to criticize Republican conservatives in terms of social morality. We Democrats reflect the best combination of personal freedom and social justice. We should study the complex history of philosophical and religious ideas that have influenced present political doctrines. Otherwise we will continue losing ground in the struggle to frame a general concept of what we stand for as the truly public spirited party.

August 11, 2005

An open letter to Wesley Clark

A Political Philosophy That Will Win Elections

Many of us Democrats look to you for a philosophical answer to the question that our leaders in Washington seem to be at a loss to deal with: "What does the Democratic Party stand for?" They respond with admirable lists of things that we are for or against, but they do not present a general political philosophy that explains our overall motives and values.

The Preamble to the Constitution implies a philosophy that distinguishes our Party from the Republicans. Certainly, as you have shown so well, we share with them a devotion to "the common defense"; but with respect to the other key terms of the Preamble, as intended for the common good, we can prove ourselves far truer to the Founding Fathers than the Republicans prove themselves to be. We have the advantage in any debate about the meanings of "a more perfect Union ... establish Justice ... insure domestic Tranquility ... promote the general Welfare ... secure the Blessings of Liberty to ourselves and our posterity ..." We can make it clear that Republicans do not measure up to Constitutional standards.

We lead in most of the polls about particular issues, but as a Party we aren't yet able to win the people's confidence in our governance because we haven't offered in plain language the general objectives that account for our apparently unconnected specific stands. We haven't yet shown what Democrats believe is the common good (even if we don't agree among ourselves on every single means for contributing to it in an open and equitable society). We must distinguish our ideas from the selfish individualism that underlies most of the unadvertised political philosophy implicit in Republicanism.

Yours is the one voice that can rally Democrats of all kinds with a political philosophy that will win elections by complementing the DNC's essential grass-root initiatives now underway. You can win the power to represent all the people, from the homeless to the richest, by *proclaiming* the answer to the question of what we stand for. As an intellectual warrior, teacher, diplomat, and businessman – a sympathetic leader and manager capable of writing your own books – who all but won your first brief political campaign as a dark horse, please continue to propound general ideas!

October 31, 2005
To local Democrats

The One Great Idea

Not for seventy-five years have the consequences of Republican political philosophy been so plain for all the world to see. This philosophy of personal and collective selfishness is not necessarily the philosophy of all who register or vote as Republicans, but by deception and sheer political power it has been imposed upon us as our government's, as representing our democracy in the estimation of the world.

In the name of individualism and free-market economy we have been led to corruption, unnecessary war, social injustice, financial folly, and perpetual crimes against Mother Earth and all her live posterity. With piteous cries against all taxes, boasts of their own competence, claims of moral virtue, promises of fiscal magic, drum rolls of single-issue patriotism, trumpeting of military force, and (perhaps above all) demands for "smaller government", they have delivered us to the edge of an almost irreversible decline in American civilization.

But it is not enough for us as Democrats to clarify what we are fighting against. Nor is it enough to list our immediate positions in resistance or initiative intended to restore an open and rationally progressive government with ultimate consideration of what we pass on to future generations of all races and classes. Of course we should always fight for the particular measures required to get a liberal recovery underway.

What we do need most to do, right now, before the next round of campaigns, is replace the Republican political philosophy with our own philosophy in the consciousness of Americans.

To start with, let's draw everyone's attention to the Preamble of the Constitution, which emphasizes the "General Welfare" (also known as the Common Good). Then we must get people to realize what that phrase means as the one great idea that underlies everything we stand for. The common good is not just "the greatest good for the greatest number". It's the best possible good – all things considered as vital parts of a single body politic. Some of the parts must moderate their own wishes; others deserve a larger share of benefit: it's the health of the whole body that should be, as the Founding Fathers meant, our political criterion – whether government is large or small, depending upon what is found by pragmatic consensus to be most expedient under present and future conditions.

With this approach to debates we can beat the Republicans, hands down, in the battle of ideas, which they themselves have been calling for in the mistaken belief that their notion of "conservatism" has been forever implanted in the hearts and minds of America.

November 7, 2005

To Manfred Hegemann

The Widening Economic Gap

Nice to hear from you!

Was there any damage nearby in the river below you during the recent floods (which didn't occur around here, although the beach, as usual, was temporarily re-shaped)?

The widening economic gap (obscured by the *average* statistics) is more and more obvious here. It started under Reagan but it's accelerated under King George. Multimillion-dollar new houses (and merely million-dollar renovations) have absorbed all the service labor, especially carpenters, for ordinary maintenance. But the gentrification is not correspondingly aesthetic. The Republican mentality everywhere you look! – in stinky old gull-ridden Gloucester!

... I hope the Washington Crats won't crow excessively over the Can vulnerability. Time is on our side – the longer all these controversies drag out before the 2006 elections the more we benefit – as long as our critics at least pretend to be judicious and open-minded, just enough to keep the pot boiling. Will you be getting a Crat governor?

April 21, 2006

Letter to editor, *American Prospect*

The Makings of a Political Philosophy

From Michael Tomasky [to the *American Prospect* Magazine, "Party in Search of a Notion"] we at last have a recognition of what we've been missing! His article has the makings of a political philosophy for Democrats – exactly the right one, just when we need it most, starting at the precinct level but especially as it may ascend to voices in Washington.

The "Common Good" is a venerable concept. In our dictionary it is equivalent to "the general Welfare" included in the Preamble to the Constitution (along with Union, Justice, Tranquility, common defense, Liberty, and Posterity).

None of the founding fathers was very happy about the Constitution itself; but it was offered as a pragmatically durable compromise, just flexible enough to afford a variety of contingencies or amendments. Those who wrote it were basically united only in a comprehensive idea of their essential purpose – their common motive – in offering a sovereign people the framework for national self-government.

What we need to debate Republicans about is all right there in the Preamble. Their collective selfishness, abuse of language, and managerial incompetence are now so pronounced that we can even discredit their exclusive boast to "provide for the common defense". Their other claims to respect for the Preamble are so weak that we can expect them to avoid as much as they can the One Big Idea that's essential to a political philosophy.

Yet the Preamble is a very brief and simple paragraph that everyone can understand and pledge to. Let us wave the truly patriotic flag of the Preamble, with the Common Good as our motto. It is the one Big Idea that can unite Democrats while discussing our internal differences – much as the founding fathers once did for the country as a whole.

May 20, 2006

To Manfred Hegemann

Worried (for 2008) about McCain

Yes indeed. What's the line between "self-reliance" and selfishness: the basic Republican philosophy on both personal and collective level?

But the theme of Common Good is appearing more and more in journalism.

And so is the idea that GWB is one of our very worst presidents; but I'm worried (for 2008) about McCain (a dyed-in-the-wool conservative) winning on false grounds.

Why do you say that neither Gore nor Clark (my two favorites) won't run? Let one of them put Hillary in the Cabinet!

As according to plan all along I'm getting a final bout of surgery on June 5. I hope the recuperation will be a little faster this time. Meanwhile I've been urgently at my writing, where I've already lost almost half a year of progress. In any case I'll have to be a (friendly) hermit until I've finished it (God willing) within another year.

April 15, 2007

Letter to editor, *Gloucester Daily Times*

Centralized Voting

Is this Florida? Is this Ohio?

Or can it be that the mayor and city clerk are proposing to discourage voters in the name of efficiency?

It may save the city clerk's department some money but it increases the costs of voters, whether in personal time or transportation costs. It certainly doesn't help the environment to raise so much extra intra-city traffic. Gloucester is a very spacious community. Rain or shine, walking will be out of the question for almost all voters. You can't expect taxi-service from downtown buses for those who have no other transportation.

Not to mention radical disruption of the school system.

Just stop to envision all the reasons for being unable or unwilling to vote, even under the best of conditions! Who will be the most affected? Who will gain the political advantage? This is a basic political issue. It is exactly parallel to recent national elections that have been decided by efforts to turn away or otherwise discourage voting.

If the city clerk is concerned about voter fraud in Gloucester he should investigate for evidence. This cry of alarm has been used and discredited in relation to cases now being investigated in Washington as a central issue in in American democracy. The overwhelming evidence indicates deliberate partisan efforts to suppress political opposition.

I hope it's only a random coincidence that this proposal happens to come at a time when the national Republican Party is under fire for tactics similar to this proposal in its efforts to suppress voting by its political opponents. I trust our officials are sincerely naive in their imagination of what it would be like in this city to implement their extremely inefficient scheme.

February 29, 2008
To Lars Hakanson

We Have Hillary

It is very pleasing to know that you'll be here this summer, assuming that your consideration means more than just 90%!

You are right to be considering Obama, because he is probably all he seems to be in intelligence, education, attitude, communication, and benign leadership – but I'm afraid he's too dangerous, right now, when we have Hillary (of your Wellesley), the extraordinary alternative. A few men in history have too easily swept their countries into moral disasters with an overconfidence in goodwill and wisdom that tends to reverse its values in the effort to avoid their personal misjudgment on behalf of a common good that they don't fully understand, until they or it are driven to anti-democratic reaction. I hope I'm wrong that this may be the result of his premature presidency, much as I've otherwise liked him – at least now that we have Hillary, who's at least as benignly extraordinary as he is in her different means toward the common good.

Chronology

1952   *Presidential election year.* On Nov. 4, Republican Dwight Eisenhower beat Democrat Adlai Stevenson in a landslide. Republicans gained control of the House and Senate.

...

1976   *Presidential election year.* On Nov. 2, Democrat Jimmy Carter narrowly won against Republican Gerald Ford. Democrats retained control of the House and Senate.

1980   *Presidential election year.* President Jimmy Carter won the Democratic nomination over Massachusetts Senator Edward Kennedy. Republican Ronald Reagan won in an Electoral College landslide on Nov. 4. Republicans gained control of the Senate for the first time since 1955.

1982   House election year during President Reagan's first term. Democrats gained seats in the House and retained their majority. Republicans retained the Senate.

1984   *Presidential election year.* Republican President Ronald Reagan gained a second term, carrying 49 states and defeating Democrat Walter Mondale. Republicans retained control of the Senate and gained House seats but Democrats had the majority.

1986   Congressional election year during President Reagan's second term. Democrats gained control of the Senate and retained their House majority.

1988   *Presidential election year.* Republican George H. W. Bush beat Democrat Michael Dukakis on Nov. 8. Democrats retained control of the House and Senate.

1990   Congressional election on Nov. 6, during the middle of
       President George H. W. Bush's term. Democrats retained
       control of the House and Senate.

1992   *Presidential election year.* Democrat Bill Clinton beat incumbent
       President George H. W. Bush on Nov. 3. Democrats retained
       control of the House and Senate. (This was the first time since
       1980 that Democrats controlled the Presidency and both
       chambers.)

1994   Congressional election during President Bill Clinton's first
       term. On Nov. 8, Republicans gained 54 House seats, their
       largest seat gain since 1946. Republicans gained control of the
       House and Senate. Republican Newt Gingrich (Georgia)
       became Speaker of the House.

1996   *Presidential election year.* President Bill Clinton beat Republican
       Bob Dole on Nov. 5, gaining a second term. Republicans
       retained control of the Senate (Trent Lott of Mississippi,
       Majority Leader) and the House.

1997   Republicans attempted to add a balanced budget amendment
       to the Constitution. They needed 67 votes. The proposed
       amendment lost by one vote in March.

1998   President Bill Clinton's sexual relationship with a White House
       intern was exposed by the press. At a January 26 press
       conference Clinton said, "I did not have sexual relations with
       that woman."

       In the Congressional elections on Nov. 3, Republicans retained
       control of the Senate and House.

1999   President Clinton delivered his State of the Union address on
       Jan. 19. On Feb. 12, the Senate acquitted Clinton in
       impeachment proceedings. On May 15, the Massachusetts
       Democratic State Convention was held in Springfield.

2000   *Presidential election year.* Vice President Al Gore ran against Senator Bill Bradley for the Democratic nomination for President. Bradley withdrew from the race on March 9.

Republican Texas governor George W. Bush ran against Alan Keys, John McCain, Steve Forbes, Gary Bauer, and Orrin Hatch for the Republican nomination.

The Nov. 7 election pitted Republican George W. Bush (Texas) against Democrat Al Gore (Tennessee) as well as Ralph Nader of the Green Party and several other small parties. The results were contested because of a close vote in Florida. If all of Florida's Nader votes had gone to Al Gore, Gore would have won Florida and the Presidency.

On Dec. 12, the U.S. Supreme Court ruled 7-2 against the Florida Supreme Court's ruling requiring a Florida recount.

The House remained in Republican control. The Senate became split 50-50 until Jeffords left the Republican Party in 2001.

2001   On Jan. 6, a joint session of Congress certified the vote and Republican George W. Bush became President-Elect.

Senator John Ashcroft (Missouri) was chosen as U.S. Attorney General by President George W. Bush.

Republican Paul O'Neill became Secretary of the Treasury.

Republican Senator Trent Lott (Mississippi) served as Majority Leader Jan. 20 – June 6.

Because of a series of changes in the composition of the Senate, Democratic Senator Tom Daschle (South Dakota) became Senate Majority Leader from June 6 through January 3, 2003.

Attacks on U.S. by al-Quaeda on Sept. 11.

2002   Congressional election during G. W. Bush's first term. On Nov.
            5, Republicans gained control of the Senate, with Trent Lott
            (Mississippi) becoming Majority Leader. The House remained
            in Republican control, with seats gained.

            In the Mass. Governor's race, Republican Mitt Romney
            defeated Democrat Shannon O'Brien.

2003   Republican President G. W. Bush ordered an invasion of Iraq in
            March.

2004   *Presidential election year.* Democratic Primary candidates were
            Carol Moseley Braun, Wesley Clark, Howard Dean, John
            Edwards, Dick Gephardt, Bob Graham, Dennis Kucinich, John
            Kerry, Joe Lieberman, Al Sharpton.

            In July, Senator John Kerry (Massachusetts) was nominated as
            the Democratic candidate for President at the Democratic
            National Convention in Boston. Illinois State Senator Barack
            Obama gave the keynote address.

            On Nov. 2, Republican George W. Bush was reelected
            President (along with Vice President Dick Cheney), beating
            Democrat John Kerry. The House and Senate remained in
            Republican control.

2006   Congressional election on Nov. 7. Democrats gained control of
            the House and Senate.

2008   *Presidential election year.* Senators Barack Obama and Hillary
            Clinton ran for the Democratic Presidential nomination.

Index

Advertising, 36, 40, 84, 90, 95, 97

Albright, Madeleine, 19, 24

American Prospect magazine, 46, 63, 75, 123

Aquinas, Thomas, 103

Ashcroft, John, 41, 42, 59

Balanced Budget Amendment, 12-15

Balkans, 80, 82, 83

Bible, 5, 7, 8, 9, 41, 61

Biden, Joe, 24, 25, 92

Blair, Tony, 40, 64, 68, 70-71, 76, 80, 81-82, 93

Boston Globe, 14, 20, 32, 42

Bradley, Bill, 23, 25-26

Bush, George H. W., 10, 11, 26

Bush, George W., 22, 23, 30, 31, 35, 38, 42-53 passim, 56-60 passim, 63, 64, 66, 70-71, 73-102 passim, 116, 119, 123, 125

Business, 60, 86, 87, 88, 94, 95, 115

Campaign finance, 26

Carter, Jimmy, 4-5, 90

Carville, James, 66

Cheney, Dick, 93

Civil rights, 27, 59, 65, 79, 113

Civil War, 42, 59

Clark, Wesley, 64, 67, 69, 70, 74, 75-76, 80-95 passim, 98, 104, 106, 118, 120, 125

Clinton, Bill, 14, 15, 18-26 passim, 35, 41, 43, 48, 49, 50, 70, 71, 72, 82, 84, 86-87, 88, 116

Clinton, Hillary, 24, 48, 84, 118, 125, 126

Common Good, 16, 20, 35, 37, 40, 46-47, 49, 50, 60, 65, 67, 71, 78, 79, 85-90 passim, 96, 101-109 passim, 112, 115-126 passim

Constitution, 13, 37, 39, 54, 92, 111-124 passim

Culture, 60, 113

Cuomo, Mario, 10

Dalrymple, Theodore, 105

Daschle, Tom, 49, 52

Davis, Gray, 45, 73

Dean, Howard, 19, 69, 70, 72, 74, 76-77, 84-92 passim, 119

Debt/deficit, 6, 12, 14, 16, 73, 84-95 passim, 106

Defense (*see* Military)

DNC (Democratic National Committee), 98, 103, 119, 121

Disarmament, 40

Dowd, Maureen, 66, 116

Dukakis, Michael, 19

Economic royalists, 13, 15, 81

Education, 40, 85, 95, 97, 113

Edwards, John, 76

Egypt, 4

Eisenhower, Dwight, 3

Electoral College, 37-38, 57, 59, 92

Environment, 13, 16, 20, 24, 26, 33, 40, 47, 50, 60, 65, 78, 79, 85-88 passim, 95-97 passim, 113, 122, 125

Europe, 19, 51, 82

Florida, 36, 38-39, 40, 56, 58, 59, 125

Forbes, Steve, 22, 23

Foreign affairs/policy, 4, 22, 23, 25, 49, 51, 60, 61, 76-83 passim, 86-92 passim, 97, 99, 101, 109, 113, 114

Founding fathers, 35, 120, 122, 124

Free trade, 46, 113

Gay marriage, 104, 105

Gender issues, 16, 57

"General Welfare," 111, 121, 122, 124

Gingrich, Newt, 12, 101

Gloucester Daily Times, 4, 26, 29, 32, 36, 37, 53, 61, 98, 101, 125

Goebbels, Joseph, 56

Goldscheider, Eric, 20

Gore, Al, 19, 20, 23, 26, 28, 35, 38, 41-52 passim, 57-76 passim, 84, 125

Graham, Bob, 70, 75, 76

Gramm, Phil, 14

Gulf War, first, 62

Gun control, 48

Hamilton, Alexander, 27

Haiti, 22

Hatch, Orrin, 57

Health care, 18, 19, 22, 27, 33, 73, 85, 113

Helms, Jesse, 24, 25

Hersh, Seymour M., 64

Hertzberg, Hendrik, 19

Hitler, 18, 104

Holbrooke, Richard, 24

Housing, 85

Human rights, 4, 16, 82, 85, 97

Hussein, Saddam, 61, 62, 92, 93

Impeachment, 17

International affairs, *see* Foreign affairs/policy

Iran-Contra, 43

Iraq, 25, 51, 61, 92, 93

Israel, 4, 5, 7, 22, 41, 48-49

Jackson, Derrick, 42

Jackson, Jesse, 41

Jefferson, Thomas, 27

Judiciary, 27, 57, 59, 65, 78

Keillor, Garrison, 58

Kennedy, Edward M., 4

Kennedy, Joseph, 86

Kennedy, Joseph P., II, 15

Kerry, John, 48, 49, 51, 59-60, 70-76 passim, 88-95 passim, 100-107 passim

Kristof, Nicholas, 73, 74

Krugman, Paul, 64, 98

Kucinich, Dennis, 70, 92

Kuttner, Robert, 75

Labor, 30, 50, 60, 114, 115

Lakoff, George, 107

Lee, Philip J., *Against the Protestant Gnostics,* 10

Lieberman, Joe, 76

Lott, Trent, 53, 59

Major, John, 10

McCain, John, 22, 28, 30, 124, 125

McGovern, George, 23

Meehan, Marty, 15

Military, 22, 49, 53, 60, 62, 78, 80, 82, 83, 85, 86, 88, 93, 96, 99, 102, 113, 114, 122

Mondale, Walter, 56
Moore, Michael, 35, 103
Muslim civilization, 61
Nader, Ralph, 36, 40, 47, 48, 98
National Security, *see* Military
NATO, 51, 82, 88
New Deal, 1, 60, 109
New York Times, 12, 32, 64, 73-77
    passim, 98
New Yorker magazine, 19, 28, 64
Nixon, Richard M., 6, 43
North Korea, 53, 61
Nuclear missiles, 61
Oak tree, Democratic, 65, 78, 111
Obama, Barack, 98, 126
O'Brien, Shannon, 56, 57
O'Neill, Paul H., 44
Pentagon, *see* Military
Popular vote, 37-38
Powell, Colin, 93
Public transportation, 113
Quayle, Dan, 22
Reagan, Ronald, 6, 11, 47, 57, 66,
    68, 86, 88, 120, 123
Rehnquist, William, 42
Robb, Chuck, 116
Robertson, Pat, 45
Romney, Mitt, 57
Roosevelt, Eleanor, 24
Roosevelt, Franklin Delano, 1, 7, 13,
    29, 35, 49, 59, 60, 70, 86, 110
Roosevelt, Teddy, 50
Rove, Carl, 75, 103, 115, 117

Rumsfeld, Donald, 93
Social Security, 42, 120
Soros, George, 103
South, 42-43, 59, 85, 87, 93
Speer, Albert, 45
States' rights, 37-39, 42, 59, 73, 85
Stevenson, Adlai, 1-3, 5, 31
Supreme Court, 14, 30, 39, 53,
    58, 66
Taxation, 12, 13, 14, 15, 26, 46,
    73, 113, 115, 122
Tawney, R. H., *Religion and the
    Rise of Capitalism,* 7, 9
Terrorism, 61
Test Ban Treaty, 20
Thatcher, Maggie, 11, 16, 68,
    120
Tomasky, Michael, 123
Television, 32, 34, 35, 40, 68, 95,
    104
Truman, Harry, 3, 35
Unions, *see* Labor
United Nations, 24-25, 40, 51,
    62, 82, 114
Ventura, Jesse, 58
Viet Nam, 49
Welfare, social, 50, 60, 81, 85,
    113
Wills, Garry, *A Necessary Evil,*
    28
Wilson, Woodrow, 1
World War II, 109
Yugoslavia, 22

About the Author

Jonathan Bayliss (1926-2009), novelist and playwright, grew up in poverty during the Great Depression in Cambridge, Massachusetts, and Vermont. He began college at Harvard but left after his freshman year to enlist in the Navy during World War II. After the war he graduated from the University of California at Berkeley.

Bayliss's novels *Prologos, Gloucesterbook, Gloucestertide,* and *Gloucestermas* make up his fiction tetralogy *Gloucesterman.* His two plays, *The Tower of Gilgamesh* and *The Acts of Gilgamesh,* form part of the novels.

Bayliss earned his livelihood in positions involved with sales analysis, accounting controls, and management, beginning in 1950 at a Berkeley bookstore. In the 1960s, as controller at Gorton's of Gloucester, the frozen-fish processor, he was a pioneer in the development of integrated business systems using an early IBM mainframe computer. Later he worked for the City of Gloucester, Massachusetts, as an aide to the mayor and as city treasurer. Bayliss was putting the finishing touches on his final novel when he died in Gloucester in 2009 at the age of 82.

Bayliss was a Democrat from youth until death. A long-time member of the Gloucester Democratic City Committee, he contributed short essays about politics to its newsletter.

If people of goodwill converge from their various but similar roots of interest, their community of values can rise like a hardy oak for all seasons, ... from acorn to winter twigs and summer leaves, generation after generation.

— *Jonathan Bayliss, 2003*